# Interstate Migration of the Elderly

# Interstate Migration of the Elderly

An Economic Analysis

Steve L. Barsby

Dennis R. Cox

**Lexington Books**
D.C. Heath and Company
Lexington, Massachusetts
Toronto          London

**Library of Congress Cataloging in Publication Data**

Barsby, Steve L.
    Interstate migration of the elderly.

    Bibliography: p.
    Includes index.
    1. Migration, Internal—United States. 2. Aged—United States. I. Cox,
Dennis R., joint author. II. Title.
HB1965.B37        301.32'6        73-11663
ISBN 0-669-87122-2

Published simultaneously in Canada.

Printed in the United States of America.

International Standard Book Number: 0-669-87122-2

Library of Congress Catalog Card Number: 73-11663

For Nina,
and for Janet

# Contents

# List of Figures

# List of Tables

# Preface

Most research concerning problems faced by elderly persons, and the policy recommendations which result, assume implicitly that the geographic distribution of older persons can be taken as a given. The general assumption seems to be that long-range policy planning can be conducted based on current age-specific population distributions, or on current rates of change in these distributions. Little consideration has been given to the possibility that implementation of policy decisions based on current population makeup may well influence the size of the population group with which those policies deal.

If the implementation of policies *does* influence the size of the "target" population, the act of carrying out the policies will change the magnitude of the problem, affect the vigor with which the policies must be pursued, and possibly create the necessity of taking other policy actions. For example, will development of low-cost housing to help the elderly in a city, county or state induce in-migration from other areas of persons attempting to take advantage of the lower-cost, more adequate housing? If so, the relevant governmental body may find itself faced with an aged population substantially larger than the initial one (that on which the size of the housing project was based), with nearly as many persons living in inadequate housing after construction has been completed as were before construction. Under these conditions, completion of the housing project might not end the pressure which originally led to its construction. Furthermore, the resulting larger population of elderly persons could increase transportation and health service needs above the levels that previously existed.

Is low-cost housing likely to have greater attraction for some elderly persons than for others? The specific economic and social impacts on the local economy of the aged in-migrants depend to a great extent on their income, age, and sex distribution. If a reasonable prediction of the number and composition of in-migrants can be made, original plans based on expected consequences of current policy actions will be better framed than those ignoring such considerations. Many policy decisions other than housing made by states and their subdivisions have implications for in- and out-migration rates of elderly persons.[a]

Assume a state decides to depend more heavily on income taxes for revenue than before, so that as time passes, per capita income taxes in that state rise relative to those in other states. Will this induce a movement of elderly persons into or out of the state? Are the aged sensitive to tax advantages in selecting where to live? Are they more or less sensitive than other age groups of the population in this respect? There are other important questions:

Will increases in old age assistance payment levels (relative to other states)

---

[a]Actually, decisions made in the public sector will influence migration rates of persons of all ages, as will decisions made in the private sector. Our present concern, however, is with migration of older age groups.

induce in-migration of elderly persons from other states? Are the elderly influenced in their migration decisions by the wage rates of jobs for which they might qualify? Are they influenced by the industrial make-up of the state?

What influence on overall migration of the elderly is a general increase in social security benefits likely to have? If migration rates increase as a result of higher benefits, how will they affect migration rates for each state? Which group(s) of the elderly is (are) most likely to increase its (their) migration rates?

This list of questions might be extended almost indefinitely. And the questions are not academic. Elderly persons' consumption patterns differ significantly from those of younger age groups, their attachment to the labor force is lower, they require relatively larger amounts of public services, etc. Differences in living patterns of the elderly compared to younger persons *must* make themselves felt on the economies of states (and cities and counties) which experience changes in the age distribution of their residents. As the elderly become a larger proportion of total population these differences in living patterns assume greater significance for planning decisions.

## Goals of the Book

This book does not attempt to answer every question posed above. It suggests possible answers for many of them, however, and in the process of arriving at these answers, we propose research avenues for reaching more definite conclusions and explore many unanswered questions. Our specific goals are:

1. to indicate the nature of the more important factors which affect interstate migration rates of the elderly,
2. to suggest which of these factors are positively related, and which are negatively related, to in- and out-migration rates,
3. to measure the relative importance of the various factors influencing migration rates,
4. to find out if different age groups of the elderly and males and females are affected differently by the various factors,
5. to identify variables which explain interstate migration rates of the elderly between 1955 and 1960 and then to test those variables' ability to explain migration rates for the period 1965 to 1970, and
6. to suggest what are likely to be the more fruitful directions of research revolving around the influences acting on migration decisions of the elderly.

In the course of our research, we also compared migration patterns of the elderly with those of younger persons, and measured some of the differences in the factors affecting movements of the elderly relative to persons under age 65. These findings are included, and provide some of the more important insights which result from this research effort.

# Acknowledgments

We wish to express our gratitude to the many people who contributed their time to this research effort. In particular, we wish to thank Evelyn Van Dyke, Marjorie Parker, Larry Davidson, and Randy Downer at the University of Arizona. Mrs. Steve Barsby prepared the majority of the final manuscript, assisted by Pamela DeCandio.

The University of Arizona and The City College of New York made their computer facilities available for our extensive computations.

Portions of this research were supported under Grant Number 10-P-56029/9-01 with the Social and Rehabilitation Service and Social Security Administration, Department of Health, Education and Welfare.

# 1 Definition of "Elderly"

This book deals with migration of "elderly" persons, a term with no single, widely used, meaning. Throughout this book we define elderly persons as those aged 65 and above. Use of "elderly" in this fashion is arbitrary, because there obviously are no definite ages when persons change from "young" to "middle age," and from "middle age" to "elderly." Economic and social characteristics associated with increasing age set in slowly and become more significant as time passes. Age 45 often is used as an arbitrary dividing line between younger and older workers, and is appropriate because many of the labor-force problems associated with increasing age become serious at about this age. It is also a convenient age to use since much of the labor-force data are presented in 5- or 10-year groupings, with age 44 ending one of these.

## Labor-Force Activity

Cross-section data indicate that overall unemployment rates begin to increase for persons aged 45 and above, and that the proportion of unemployed persons experiencing long-term unemployment is higher among older than among younger workers. Labor-force participation rates for males begin to decrease between age 35 and 45, those for females between age 45 and 55.[1]

Withdrawals from the labor force begin well before age 65. In fact, the number of males not in the labor force in 1970 nearly doubles from 394,000 for those aged 40-44 to 636,000 for those aged 55-59.[2] The number of males employed full time falls by some 26 percent from 4.8 million in the younger age group to 3.5 million in that aged 55-59. Since the numbers of males employed part time, not working but having a job, and unemployed, remain virtually constant between these age groups 40-44 and 55-59, the rate of withdrawal from the labor force about matches that at which the number of males employed full time declines.

Significant changes in these trends occur, however, in later years. After declining slowing but steadily for some years, the number of males employed part time suddenly begins increasing; the number of males with a job but not working reverses its long trend upward and begins declining; and the number unemployed decreases more rapidly than before. At the same time, the rate of

1

withdrawal from the labor force increases as does the rate of decline in the number of males employed full time. All these trends suggest that withdrawal from the labor force by males proceeds at a rather steady pace until around age 60, at which time males exit from the labor force at an increasingly rapid rate.[a] Thus while age 65 may be the predominant single retirement age, significant numbers of males withdraw from the labor force prior to age 65 with large numbers of these withdrawals coming between ages 60 and 65.

### Migration

Even though significant changes in labor-force attachment occur following age 55, migration rates display a remarkable stability and regularity until persons reach their early 60s, then migration rates begin climbing rapidly. These rates for the two periods 1955-1960 and 1965-1970 are contained in Table 1-1. Mobility rates between 1955 and 1960 of persons aged 55 to 64 in 1960 vary by only .003 (.040 to .043).[b] Beginning with those reaching age 64 in that year, rates increase successively for older ages to a high of .046 for those aged 67 in 1960. Not until age 71 do mobility rates fall to the lower levels associated with ages 58 through 64.

Similar migration rates over the period 1965-1970 display the same general patterns of those a decade earlier, but rates for persons under age 63 and over age 65 are lower. Instead of rates between .040 and .043 for persons aged 55 to 62, rates range between .034 and .038. Then they rise more rapidly, hitting the same peak of .046, but at age 66 rather than age 67. Following age 65, rates in the latter period again are below those for 1955-1960 for each age group. We can offer no explanation for the generally lower migration rates among the "younger" persons between 1965 and 1970 as compared to those for 1955 to 1960. The peaking of the rate a year earlier might be due to a fall in the average retirement age.[c] With this displacement to the left of the migration "curve" by age, we then would expect such rates to be higher as we approach age 65, and lower following that age group.

While Figure 1-1 accompanying Table 1-1 overemphasizes the differences in mobility among various age groups, it seems clear that a notable change in

[a] Our concentration of attention on labor-force behavior of males is not meant to suggest that such behavior of females may be ignored. Trends discussed above have changed only little for many years, however, while major changes are occurring in the levels and timing of labor-force entry and exit of females. Observations for 1970 may no longer be relevant in 1980.

[b] Since migration is measured as a flow—in this case over a five-year period—we cannot identify the specific age at which migration occurred.

[c] Trends in labor-force participation rates support this supposition. For the age group 60 to 64, the participation rate of males fell from .82 in 1960 to .75 in 1970.

mobility patterns begins to emerge for those reaching about age 65 in 1960 (and in 1970).[d]

## Retirement and Migration

Our primary interest revolves around migration rates, with a focus on migration patterns resulting from decisions other than those presumed to be associated with a high degree of attachment to the labor force. Consequently, while we recognize that decreasing labor-force attachment begins some thirty years earlier, our definition of elderly is based on the relatively sudden change in migration rates around age 65. Two additional considerations for selecting age 65 should not be ignored.

First, 65 is the traditional retirement age for social security and private pension plans. A large number of persons can be expected to retire right at age 65 because of income provisions contained in these plans. Second, since we concentrate on migration over a five-year period, and since we have seen that withdrawals from the labor force accelerate around age 60, selection of persons reaching age 65 in 1960 (or 1970) allows us to include in our study persons who retire between ages 60 and 65.[e]

Our continuing reference throughout the book to those aged 65 and above as the "elderly," or the "aged," thus is not meant to suggest that upon turning 65, persons suddenly change from young to old. The terms simply are shorthand ways of referring to our study group—a more or less well-defined group of persons generally characterized by substantially decreased attachment to the labor force and diminished incomes, and by mobility patterns that may be

[d]The combination of trends discussed above—a gradual, then increased rate of withdrawal from labor-force activity followed only some years later by significantly increased migration rates—suggests that much of the decreased labor-force participation of males between the ages of 40 and 60 is involuntary. If withdrawal were voluntary, i.e., if retirement decisions were being made, one should see increases in migration rates accompanying the increased rates of withdrawal from the labor force. Since this is not observed, males must be leaving the labor force reluctantly and hoping to re-enter should jobs become available. Only when they reach "retirement" age do they make their decision to migrate.

This supposition of non-voluntary labor-force withdrawal is supported by William Bowen and T. Aldrich Finegan (*The Economics of Labor Force Participation* [Princeton: Princeton University Press, 1969] p. 343), who find that a 1 percentage point increase in the unemployment rate of males aged 55-64 is associated with a fall of 1.49 percentage points in their labor-force participation rate compared to a .32 percentage point reduction for males aged 25-54. Since unemployment rates rise as people age, substantial labor-force withdrawal among workers nearing age 65 must occur. In fact, the relatively strong reaction of older males to increases in unemployment rates is one of the reasons why such rates are as low as they are. Rather than remain in the labor force as unemployed persons, they leave the labor force and are no longer "unemployed."

[e]Problems associated with using a five-year period for measuring migration are discussed below in Chapters 2 and 3.

**Table 1-1**
**Migration Rates for Persons Aged 55 and Over, by Individual Age,[a] 1955-1960 and 1965-1970**

| Age | Migration Rate | |
|---|---|---|
| | 1955-1960 | 1965-1970 |
| 55 | .041 | .037 |
| 56 | .043 | .036 |
| 57 | .042 | .035 |
| 58 | .041 | .035 |
| 59 | .040 | .034 |
| 60 | .040 | .035 |
| 61 | .040 | .036 |
| 62 | .041 | .038 |
| 63 | .040 | .041 |
| 64 | .041 | .041 |
| 65 | .042 | .044 |
| 66 | .045 | .046 |
| 67 | .046 | .045 |
| 68 | .045 | .044 |
| 69 | .044 | .042 |
| 70 | .043 | .039 |
| 71 | .041 | .038 |
| 72 | .038 | .037 |
| 73 | .038 | .036 |
| 74 | .036 | .033 |
| 75 | .034 | .033 |

[a]Age in 1960 and in 1970.
Source: U.S. Department of Commerce, Bureau of the Census, *U.S. Census of Population, 1960: Subject Reports, Mobility for States and State Economic Areas*, Final Report PC (2)-2B (Washington, D.C.: Government Printing Office, 1962), Table 24. U.S. Department of Commerce, Bureau of the Census, *U.S. Census of Population, 1970: Subject Reports, Mobility for States and the Nation*, Final Report PC (2)-2B (Washington, D.C.: Government Printing Office, 1973), Table 2.

determined by influences distinctly different from those affecting other population groups.

Consideration of the elderly as a group independently from other population segments is made more important because older persons are distributed unevenly throughout the United States, a distribution influenced substantially by recent migration. This uneven distribution of older persons among the states can be seen in Table 1-2, which contains states having either the highest or the lowest proportions of over-65 populations.

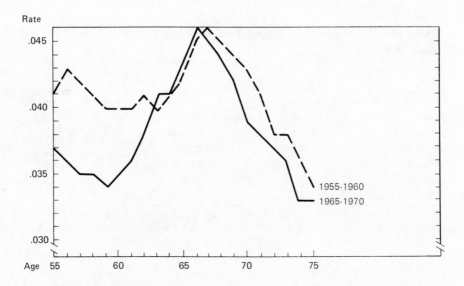

**Figure 1-1.** Migration Rates by Individual Age, 1955-1960, and 1965-1970. Source: Table 1-1.

While older persons comprised 9.9 percent of the total U.S. population in 1970, Florida's population of persons aged 65 and over made up 14.6 percent of its total population, more than six times as high as the state with the lowest such percentage (Alaska at 2.3 percent). Of course, just because a state's population has a high proportion of older persons, it does not follow that net migration of older persons to that state is positive. In fact, between 1960 and 1970, Iowa and Missouri were experiencing net *out*-migration of this age group; net in-migration rates of older persons into Nebraska and South Dakota were relatively low—1.6 percent and 0.8 percent respectively. In these states, younger persons were migrating away fast enough to make the elderly portion of the population relatively more important.

An understanding of migration patterns is thus important because a relatively large population of older persons resulting from their rapid in-migration will have different implications for a state's economy than that same population resulting from rapid out-migration of younger persons—a growth of the elderly population as a residual, so to speak.

### Preview

Chapter 2 surveys earlier studies concerned with migration of elderly persons, and finds that such research is rare. Studies examining migration of the aged

**Table 1-2**

**States with the Highest and Lowest Percentages of Populations Aged 65 and Over, 1970**

| Highest | | Lowest | |
|---|---|---|---|
| State | Percentage | State | Percentage |
| Florida | 14.6% | Alaska | 2.3% |
| Iowa | 12.4 | Hawaii | 5.7 |
| Nebraska | 12.4 | Nevada | 6.3 |
| Arkansas | 12.4 | New Mexico | 6.9 |
| Missouri | 12.0 | Utah | 7.3 |
| South Dakota | 12.1 | South Carolina | 7.4 |

Source: U.S. Bureau of the Census, *Current Population Reports*, Series P-23, No. 43, "Some Demographic Aspects of Aging in the United States" (Washington, D.C.: U.S. Government Printing Office, 1973), Table 10, p. 12.

often do so as a peripheral question, and usually contain significant data and geographic limitations which limit the generality of their conclusions.

Chapter 3 defines in more detail the scope of this book, discusses the limitations resulting from the methodology employed, introduces the migration rates used throughout our research, and describes in more detail some interesting aspects of migration patterns of the elderly.

Chapters 4 through 8 examine the influences of five groups of variables on gross in-migration, gross out-migration, and net migration rates of persons aged 65 and above, persons aged 65-69, and persons aged 64 and below between 1955 and 1960. Movements of males and females, as well as those of total population groups, are examined. Past migration rates, incomes, labor-force characteristics, and several miscellaneous variables are seen to exert substantial influences on migration patterns of all age groups and to act in different ways on elderly persons than on younger persons. Influences of the public sector (e.g., expenditures by state and local governments on public welfare) seem to have only minor impact on migration decisions.

In Chapter 9, we select eight variables from the 63 originally included, and examine the ability of those variables to explain interstate migration rates over the period 1965 through 1970. A high degree of stability in both gross migration rates and in the factors influencing those rates is found.

Chapter 10 summarizes results of earlier chapters, points out policy implications which emerge, and suggests ways in which this preliminary research might best be further pursued.

## Notes

1. U.S., Department of Commerce, Bureau of the Census, *U.S. Census of Population, 1960*, Final Report, PC (2)-6A, *Subject Reports, Employment Status and Work Experience* (Washington, D.C.: U.S. Government Printing Office, 1973), Table 1 and Table 17.

2. Ibid.

# 2

## Previous Migration Studies

The literature dealing with patterns and determinants of population mobility is massive. Most of this published research, however, concentrates on population movements as a whole, or on movements of the labor force. Research directed primarily at migration patterns of the elderly is extremely scarce.

This lack of methodical mobility studies of the elderly is understandable. Persons over age 65 are a relatively small, though growing, proportion of total population; interest in total population movements, or in movements of the labor force (never identifying explicitly the elderly) may seem to carry a higher priority. Mobility rates of persons aged 65 and over are substantially below those of younger age groups, so that movements of the elderly are a possibly less significant aspect of studies of this age group than for other age groups. A possibly more important reason than the first two may well be the absence of a well-developed theory of migration of the elderly.

While labor theory provides a compact theoretical framework (and consequently a set of a priori hypotheses which can be tested empirically) with which to examine migration patterns of the labor force, this framework is lacking for migration of older persons. Given the looser attachment of the elderly to the labor force, the elderly may well migrate in response to substantially different "signals" than younger persons, so that the theory applicable to the labor force may not apply to the elderly. Yet no alternative framework relating to the elderly has been developed.

Given the absence of a theoretical framework with which to study migration of the aged, most mobility studies of this age group simply describe migration patterns, giving little or no insight into the forces determining mobility patterns.[1] The few studies which have attempted to isolate factors affecting mobility generally have had geographic or sample size limitations which seriously limit the generality of resulting conclusions.

Some of what is known about the determinants of elderly mobility patterns has come as a side benefit of research aimed primarily at answering other questions, such as whether there are differences in social views between elderly migrants and non-migrants; or whether there are differences in labor-force attachment rates of the elderly among different geographic areas. Still, a number of factors which may affect migration rates of the elderly have been examined at one time or another, and do add insight into the forces acting on the location choice of older persons. For convenience, these factors (or variables) can be classified into the following categories:

9

1. family and social attachment
2. health and climate
3. home ownership
4. location at time of retirement (rural, suburb, central city)
5. job opportunity
6. income (both pre- and post-retirement)
7. labor-force status
8. occupation prior to retirement and educational level.

These factors clearly cover a wide range of forces, and as a whole they may encompass most of those which are measurable and act to determine whether an older person moves, and the locational choice if a move is made. The general findings of earlier studies as they relate to the above variables follow.

**Family and Social Attachment**

Without any knowledge of migration patterns, one might hypothesize that elderly persons will prefer to live in a familiar social environment, so that social ties which build up prior to retirement reduce the tendency for elderly persons to migrate following retirement. On the other hand, if a person's friends and relatives have moved in the past, greater pressures will act to induce a retired person to migrate, and to migrate to a location where acquaintances or relatives have moved previously.

This supposition (that attachment to family and friends may act to reduce out-migration of the elderly) is supported by Harold Geist in a 1965 study.[2] He finds that about 80 percent of those who retired and chose to stay in the community where they were working at the time of retirement did so because they wanted to remain in long-established social groupings, and because they were familiar with their current environment and were unwilling to risk moving into one with unknown (or partly known) characteristics.

Marilyn Langford, who developed a national sample from OASI data of about 5,000 persons, was interested directly in the impact of social contact on migration of the elderly.[3] She notes that unless a great deal of time has elapsed since the last move, elderly persons have more social contacts with relatives than with friends; and that the desire to live near families is even stronger than that to locate near community and health facilities and services. Given this strong preference to reside near relatives and friends, Langford concludes that those elderly persons with a large number of personal contacts will be less willing to move than those with fewer personal contacts.

Thus, available evidence suggests that increased social ties and mobility of the aged are negatively related if these ties are with persons in the same community, and that ties with persons in other communities increases out-migration. Of

course, these relationships probably hold for all population age groups. One might have the expectation, however, that these are stronger for older, than for younger persons.

## Health and Climate

Health and climate really are two separate variables acting independently on migration rates of the elderly. While poor health may reduce an elderly person's ability to move to another state (or community), it also creates an increased pressure to move if a different climate is expected to improve health. Thus, two types of migration might be expected to be associated with climate—one resulting because a change in climate is prescribed as a health measure, and another occurring because of personal preferences for one climate over another.

Findings (both from "casual" and coordinated research) of a number of studies are consistent with the above discussion. Poor health clearly must act as a deterrent to mobility. Yet Geist indicates that health and climate were most often given as reasons for out-migration,[4] and P.D. Simkins finds that health and climate are the most important reasons given for in-migration to Arizona.[5] Health and climate probably are extremely important reasons for a good portion of total in-migration of many states in the southern half of the United States. As of now, the conflicting influences of health (in making migration more difficult, but often more compelling) have not been measured.

## Home Ownership

As with health, one might hypothesize that the influence of home ownership on migration of the elderly is mixed. A house represents a fixed asset which may be difficult to convert into liquid assets. As such, it tends to "tie" a retired person to an area and reduce mobility. On the other hand, liquid assets are provided when a house is sold. Since receipt of income from these assets is not dependent upon a person remaining in any given location, its receipt should increase mobility.

Several studies examined by us conclude that home ownership *does* retard mobility among the aged. S.B. Prasad and Alton C. Johnson, in a study of mobility of retired industrial workers, find that only 3 percent of those owning houses moved after retiring; but that 15 percent of those not owning houses moved.[6] Langford also finds that home ownership reduces mobility. Owners responded that they were unwilling to move out of their neighborhoods more often than did renters.[7]

The possibility that the sale of a house may stimulate migration is supported by John Lansing and Eva Mueller. They find a small, but positive, simple correlation between liquid assets and mobility.[8] Of course the liquid assets may come from many sources other than the sale of a home, and the simple correlation does not guarantee that liquid assets would continue to be significant in a multiple regression equation.

## Location at Time of Retirement

It is not clear what influence residency location (city, suburb, rural) might have on migration rates of aged persons. Since the most rapidly growing portion of the population resides in suburban areas, more persons must be migrating just to get there than is the case for other locations. Thus, more persons living in suburban areas will have a history of migration than persons in either rural or city locations.

If past migration practices influence current decisions (Prasad and Johnson suggest that they do), one might expect elderly persons living in suburbs to migrate more often upon retirement than those in other locations.

Charles R. Manley finds that this is indeed the case. While his comparison of mobility rates does not include a rural classification, he finds that persons living in suburbs are more likely to move upon retirement than those in the central city.[9] Indirect evidence from Lansing and Mueller indicates the same phenomenon is occurring in all broad geographic regions (classified by population density) of the United States. Out-migration rates from areas characterized as being neither metropolitan nor rural-farm were by far the highest of the three density classifications for family heads aged 35 and over. While the elderly were only a part of this group, the rate differentials—7.8 percent, 8.4 percent, and 19.1 percent for Standard Metropolitan Statistical Areas (SMSAs), rural-farm, and "neither" respectively—are so great as to suggest that elderly from the last area were out-migrating at a faster rate than those in other areas.

While studies indicate that persons in suburban areas may be more likely to move upon retirement than those in city or rural settings, the causes of this differential in mobility rates have yet to be isolated. It may well be that those living in suburban areas are those who have a higher history of past migration and fewer family and social ties to retard their geographic movements. Higher past incomes of those in suburban areas (relative to persons in city and rural areas) probably also contribute to the observed differentials in mobility rates. At this point, however, these suggestions are only conjecture.

## Job Opportunity

Gary Becker has developed a model of migration based on the concept of human capital.[10] In Becker's framework, the opportunity to increase the present value

of future earnings induces persons to migrate. As people grow older, this capitalized value of earnings falls, so that the potential gains from moving and the stimulus to move decrease accordingly. Thus while older persons may move in response to job opportunities, we would predict that migration from this cause will fall with age.

A reduced capability to increase earnings may act to lower migration rates of the elderly, but migration in order to take the type of job "I've always wanted" may somewhat mitigate the influence of lower capitalized values of earnings. Given that the elderly as a group are relatively less dependent upon wage income than younger persons, the income aspect of taking a specific job should be relatively less important.[a]

When the Bureau of Business Services at Arizona State University surveyed recent migrant retirees in Arizona, it found that while health and climate were given as the two most important reasons for moving, job opportunity ranked third.[11] Another questionnaire study by Simkins achieved similar results. In Simkins' study, nearly 50 percent of the respondents indicated economic reasons for migrating to Arizona.[12]

At this point all one can conclude from past studies is that job opportunities might have some influence on migration decisions of the elderly, but little is known of its relative importance in the migration decision.

### Income

Migration is not free. Out-of-pocket costs of moving, temporary expenses incurred while finding a permanent residence, and costs of liquidating fixed assets are examples of expenses associated with moving. Since persons with higher incomes should be more able to bear these costs, we would expect migration rates of the elderly to be positively associated with their post-retirement incomes.

### *Census Data*

Census data indicate that migration rates of families with heads aged 65 and over and moderate income levels (incomes between $1,000 and $4,000 annually), are relatively higher than for families with extremely low or higher income levels. Table 2-1 contains a tabulation which illustrates this. In this table, if an income

---

[a]Although wage incomes are relatively less important to elderly than to younger persons, it does not follow that income can be neglected as a factor of migration by the aged. Since total incomes usually fall drastically upon "retirement," wage earnings from part-time (or part-year) employment can make important contributions to total incomes and thus might be important.

Table 2-1
Family Income and Relative Mobility Status of Persons Aged 65 and Above[a]

| Income Level | Relative Probability of Migrant Status[b] |
|---|---|
| Under $1,000 | 0.83 |
| $ 1,000 - 1,999 | 1.10 |
| 2,000 - 2,999 | 1.25 |
| 3,000 - 3,999 | 1.18 |
| 4,000 - 4,999 | 1.00 |
| 5,000 - 5,999 | 0.86 |
| 6,000 - 6.999 | 0.83 |
| 7,000 - 9,999 | 0.80 |
| 10,000 - 14,999 | 0.80 |
| 15,000 + | 0.75 |

[a]Counts all intercounty moves.

[b]Proportion of movers in each income class divided by the proportion of non-movers in each income class.

Source: Calculated from John B. Lansing and Eva Mueller, *The Geographic Mobility of Labor* (Ann Arbor: Survey Research Center, The University of Michigan, 1967), Table 28, p. 86, citing U.S., Department of Commerce, Bureau of the Census, *U.S. Census of Population, 1960: Subject Reports, Mobility of States and State Economic Areas*, Final Report PC(2)-2B (Washington, D.C.: U.S. Government Printing Office, 1962), p. 30.

group contains a higher proportion of total "movers" than of "non-movers," the statistic in that income group will exceed unity. If the proportion of non-movers exceeds that of movers, the statistic will be less than unity. Inspection of Table 2-1 reveals that higher proportions of movers are found in the income brackets between $1,000 and $3,999 than are non-movers. More non-movers, however, are in the higher income brackets than are movers, as is the case for persons with annual incomes under $1,000.

*Questionnaire Data*

Lansing and Mueller's data reflect national data and include intercounty as well as interstate migration between 1955 and 1960. A more (geographically) restricted study utilizes interviews with retired persons who lived in "retirement" communities in Florida and Wisconsin as a sample, and suggests a somewhat different conclusion than do census data.[13] Table 2-2 contains two sets of income distribution comparisons—one between Wisconsin retirees and Florida retirees who migrated there from another state, the other between Wisconsin retirees and *winter* Florida residents. Columns 2 and 3 in Table 2-2

**Table 2-2**

**Differences in Frequency Distribution of Retirees, by Income Group**

| Income | Wisconsin Retirees vs. Florida Retirees | Wisconsin Retirees vs. Winter Florida Residents |
|---|---|---|
| Under $3,000 | −22.1 | −30.3 |
| $ 3,000 - 3,999 | 11.1 | .6 |
| 4,000 - 4,999 | 1.1 | 1.7 |
| 5,000 - 5,999 | 1.9 | 1.3 |
| 6,000 - 6,999 | 1.5 | 9.9 |
| 7,000 - 7,999 | 3.0 | 9.7 |
| 8,000 - 9,999 | 0.1 | − .3 |
| 10,000+ | 2.7 | 14.8 |
| Unknown | 0.7 | −7.3 |

Source: Calculated from James S. Honnen, William I.A. Eteng, and Douglas G. Marshall, *Retirement and Migration in the North Central States, Comparative Socioeconomic Analysis: Wisconsin and Florida*, Population Series No. 19 (Madison: Department of Rural Sociology, College of Agriculture and Life Sciences, University of Wisconsin, 1969), Table 14, p. 32.

were computed by subtracting the proportion of Wisconsin retirees in each income group from similar proportions of Florida retirees, and from winter Florida residents. If the proportion of Wisconsin retirees in any income group exceeds (is less than) that in the comparable Florida income group, the statistic is negative (positive). Since all respondents living in Florida are migrants, they are all "movers."[b]

We do not know if all of the Wisconsin retirees are (interstate) non-movers, because retirees in Wisconsin are not identified by state of origin. Our own data, however, reveal that Wisconsin's gross in-migration rate of persons aged 65 and above between 1955 and 1960 ranked thirty-fourth among all the states (.024). It might be inferred, then, that the great majority of Wisconsin's retirees lived in Wisconsin prior to retirement and can be classified as (interstate) non-movers. Consequently, by comparing the differences in income distributions of Florida and Wisconsin retirees, a comparison is being made between income distributions of movers and non-movers. The only income bracket containing more non-movers than movers is that of annual incomes under $3,000. Unlike the census data presented by Lansing and Mueller, relatively more movers have annual incomes of $10,000 or over than do non-movers.

Even more indicative of a possible income bias in census migration data is a comparison of the income distributions of Wisconsin retirees and winter Florida residents (Table 2-2, last column.) Elderly persons who annually migrate between two residences have incomes that are even more skewed toward higher

[b]In making the following comparisons, it must be kept in mind that the time period over which migration is measured is indefinite in this latter study.

income brackets than Florida retirees. Census migration data do not detect these frequent movements of this group of high income persons. Since the Census is taken in May, many persons who move between summer and winter homes annually would already have moved back to their summer home at the time the Census is taken. They would be counted as non-migrants.[c] This suggests, then, that census data systematically understate the movement of high-income elderly persons.[d]

Evidence from other studies, while fragmentary, is consistent with the proposition that there is a positive relationship between income of the elderly and their mobility. Manley, in his survey of retired department store personnel, found a positive relationship between post-retirement income and mobility.[14] And the survey conducted by the Bureau of Business Services in Arizona found that in-migrants to Arizona had higher incomes than persons already living in Arizona.[15]

As with many of the other variables discussed, available evidence is inconclusive concerning the impact of post-retirement income on migration rates of the aged. The form and timing of data collection seems to be a critical factor. It does seem clear, however, that annual income below $3,000 (in 1960) greatly retards migration.

## Labor Force Participation

Earlier studies have found that participation in the labor force reduces the mobility of elderly persons. This is expected. Since older persons tend to experience relatively long periods of unemployment between jobs, quitting a job to move to a new area involves a high risk that an extended period of unemployment (and reduced income) will result.

Sidney Goldstein cites a work by A.R. Miller which examines interstate migration of persons 65 and older between 1955 and 1960. Miller finds that of the white males moving during this period, 19 percent were in the labor force as compared to an average participation rate of 31 percent for all persons aged 65 and above. After controlling for marital status, he finds that labor-force participation rates of persons migrating in each of three other subgroups of the elderly (white females, and black males and females) are below the participation rates of persons not migrating.[16] Similar findings are reported elsewhere. The Metropolitan Life Insurance Company notes that between 1957 and 1958, 11.3

[c]In the cases where the annual moves began between the two census dates over which migration is measured (May 1955 and May 1960), persons will be counted as having made one move.

[d]Actually, census data tend to understate migration of *all* age groups in *all* income brackets, a tendency discussed in more detail in Chapter 3. The particular pattern of annual movements characterizing many elderly persons with high incomes, however, is especially difficult for census data to detect.

percent of males aged 65 and over who were not in the labor force moved, while only 6.4 percent of such males in the labor force moved.[17] Goldstein finds that not only are older persons not in the labor force more likely to move, but they are more likely to move between counties, and between non-contiguous states than are their counterparts in the labor force.[18]

In their study of the determinants of labor force participation, William Bowen and Aldrich Finegan find a strong association between participation in the labor force and immobility among older persons. In a set of multiple regression equations in which they control for a number of characteristics,[e] they find an inverse relationship between labor-force participation rates and net migration rates. This inverse relationship holds for all males, single males, all females, and single females.[19]

Past evidence concerning the impact of labor force participation is quite consistent. Participation in the labor force seems to reduce mobility of elderly persons.

## Occupation Prior to Retirement, and Education

Not much has been written concerning the influence of education and occupation on the migration decision of elderly persons. Lansing and Mueller note that both higher education and skill levels are associated with higher migration rates among the elderly. Gordon Bultena and Vivian Wood cross-classify migrants and non-migrants in Arizona and Florida by broad educational categories and by occupations.[20] Their findings support those of Lansing and Mueller's. Sixty-three percent of the migrants versus 81 percent of the non-migrants received 12 or fewer years of education, and a similarly larger percentage of migrants were college graduates.

Not only had larger percentages of migrants received more years of education than non-migrants, but larger percentages of migrants were concentrated in the professional (17 percent for migrants vs. 11 percent for non-migrants) and managerial (27 percent vs. 12 percent) occupations prior to retirement. Lower percentages of migrants were found in blue collar (37 percent vs. 55 percent) and farm (6 percent vs. 11 percent) occupations. Since earnings prior to retirement will be related to the occupational breakdown used by Bultena and Wood, the results also confirm other findings that persons with higher income prior to retirement are more likely to move after retirement than are those with lower earnings histories.

---

[e]Controlled for are the unemployment rate, total earnings of males, industry mix, labor supply of older males, income other than earnings, occupational mix, years of schooling, race, and marital status.

## Conclusions

Results from the examination of earlier studies of factors affecting migration of the elderly hold few surprises. Elderly persons with many social and family attachments are more reluctant movers than those with few social or family ties. Low incomes probably reduce mobility simply because of the costs involved in moving, and possibly because persons with low incomes receive non-income assistance from friends and relatives which would be lost were an interstate move made. Expected long periods of unemployment may explain why older persons who are attached to the labor force are reluctant to leave a job and move.

High mobility among older persons is concentrated among those who have moderate income levels, live in suburban areas, are well educated, and held managerial or professional positions prior to retirement.

Much of the evidence supporting these conclusions, however, is very weak. Questionnaires developed from a non-random sampling of five or six retirement communities, or of retirees from one midwest firm, can hardly be regarded as conclusive, nor can generalizations from the results safely be made. A second serious deficiency of these studies is that they identify (for the most part) only simple associations between individual characteristics and mobility. Interrelationships among characteristics affecting mobility are largely ignored. Consequently, while one might conclude that elderly persons who had completed college, worked in managerial or professional occupations, lived in suburban areas, and have moderate incomes are more mobile than their counterparts without these characteristics, the relative contribution to mobility made by any one of these characteristics is not known. Also unknown is how mobility is affected by incremental changes in these characteristics.

## Notes

1. See, for example, Henry S. Shyrock, Jr., *Population Mobility within the United States* (University of Chicago: Community and Family Study Center, 1964), and Ann Ratner Miller, *Net Intercensal Migration to Large Urban Areas of the United States* (Philadelphia: University of Pennsylvania, Population Studies Center, May 1964).

2. Harold Giest, *The Psychological Aspects of Retirement* (Springfield, Ill.: Charles C. Thomas, Publisher, 1968).

3. Marilyn Langford, *Community Aspects of Housing for the Aged* (Ithaca, N.Y.: Center for Housing and Environmental Studies, Cornell University, 1962).

4. Geist, *Psychological Aspects*.

5. P.D. Simkins, "Regional Differences in the Recent Migration to Arizona," an abstract in *Association of American Geographers* 52 (Summer 1962), p. 360.

6. S.B. Prasad and Alton C. Johnson, "Residential Mobility of the Retired Industrial Worker," *Land Economics* 40, 2 (May 1964): 221-22.

7. Langford, *Community Aspects*, p. 27.

8. John B. Lansing and Eva Mueller, *The Geographic Mobility of Labor* (Ann Arbor, Mich.: Survey Research Center, Institute for Social Research, University of Michigan Press, 1967), pp. 190-92.

9. Charles R. Manley, "The Migration of Older People," *American Journal of Sociology* 59 (1954): 324-31.

10. Gary S. Becker, *Human Capital* (New York: National Bureau of Economic Research, 1964).

11. Bureau of Business Services, *Study of Migration* (Tempe, Ariz.: Arizona State University, 1958).

12. P.D. Simkins, "Regional Differences in the Recent Migration to Arizona," an abstract in *Association of American Geographers*, 52 (Summer 1962): 360. Simkins' results are difficult to interpret, since many of his respondents had moved prior to retirement, and since economic reasons include costs of living as well as incomes.

13. James S. Honnen, William I.A. Eteng, and Douglas G. Marshall, "Retirement and Migration in the North Central States," Population Series No. 19, *Comparative Socioeconomic Analysis, Wisconsin and Florida* (Madison: Department of Rural Sociology, College of Agricultural and Life Sciences, University of Wisconsin, 1969).

14. "Migration of Older People."

15. Bureau of Business Services, *Study of Migration*.

16. Sidney Goldstein, "Socio-Economic and Migration Differentials between the Aged in the Labor Force and in the Labor Reserve," *The Gerontologist* 7, 1 (March 1967): 31-40, citing A.R. Miller, "Migration Differentials in Labor Force Participation: United States, 1960," *Demography* 3 (1966): 58-67.

17. *Metropolitan Life Statistics Bulletin*, "Living Arrangements and Mobility of the Aged," 41 (August 1960): 6-8.

18. Goldstein, "Socio-Economic and Migration Differentials," p. 38.

19. William G. Bowen and T. Aldrich Finegan, *The Economics of Labor Force Participation* (Princeton, N.J.: Princeton University Press, 1969), p. 336, Table 10-1.

20. Gordon Bultena and Vivian Wood, "Normative Attitudes Toward the Aged Role Among Migrant and Nonmigrant Retirees," *The Gerontologist* 9, 3 (Autumn 1969): 204-08.

# 3 Scope of the Study

In what we hope is only the first phase of our investigations, we have imposed three interrelated limits on the scope of our efforts: .

1. only interstate migration of elderly persons is considered;
2. only readily available, published data are used;
3. only simple, frequently used techniques of data analysis are employed.

This chapter explores these limitations and points out their implications for interpreting our results.

## Interstate Migration

### Data Handling Problems

The principal reason for concentrating on interstate migration rather than, say, migration among SMSAs, is the magnitude of the data-handling problems associated with analysis of smaller geographic units. There are only 48 states (we have excluded Alaska and Hawaii because of lack of data). There are more than 200 SMSAs, more than 300 State Economic Areas, several hundred incorporated cities, and more than 3,000 counties in the United States. Selection of states for analysis, therefore, results in substantial savings of resources required to assemble and process statistical information. Since this work is intended as the first of a series of studies on migration of older persons, starting with states as the geographic areas seems reasonable.

### Data Availability

Another reason for the use of state data is that many types of information which are relevant in a migration study are not available for some of the smaller geographic units. This is true of the migration statistics themselves as well as statistics of other characteristics of areas which might be associated with migration. For example, previous migration rates and income data by age are not available for geographic units smaller than states. But use of state data prevents us from utilizing many variables which we think might influence migration significantly. Cost of living and population density are two of these.

*Excluded Migration*

The most important implication of this geographic limitation for mobility research is that movement within these states is ignored. Of all elderly persons who lived in different counties in 1960 than they did in 1955, only 47 percent also lived in different states. Thus more elderly movers are excluded from consideration than are included. The comparable figure for the population as a whole (persons five years of age and older) is 52 percent.[1]

Furthermore, some intrastate moves actually cover longer distances and include greater changes in environment than some interstate moves. For example, movement from Texarkana, Texas, to El Paso, Texas, is intrastate migration which is ignored in this study, while movement from Texarkana, Texas, to Texarkana, Arkansas, is interstate migration, with which this study deals. However, concentration on interstate migration does allow us to deal mainly with long-distance movement since 67 percent of all interstate movement of elderly persons between 1955 and 1960 was between non-contiguous states. (The comparable figure for all ages is 66 percent.)[2]

## Data Characteristics

The main reason for using only published data is the saving of resources. Relevant data could be obtained in other ways, but only at substantially greater cost. For example, there are innumerable tabulations of the basic census information which could be performed. For obvious reasons, the Census Bureau publishes only a small fraction of these. While the marginal cost of an additional tabulation is undoubtedly low in comparison to the total cost of the Bureau's operations, these costs would be very high in comparison to the total resources committed to preliminary research such as this.

Another type of unpublished data which might be used in a work of this nature is survey research statistics. The assembly of a substantial body of such data requires, however, teams of interviewers, coders, tabulators, etc. In order to keep down the cost of this research effort we have eschewed such undertakings.

The use of published data has a number of important implications for our research; these are discussed below.

*Aggregates*

All readily available figures on migration deal with substantial aggregates. Thus one cannot identify and account for the behavior of individuals. Personal characteristics which are most often associated with "movers" and those which are associated most often with "non-movers" cannot confidently be identified.

We find, for example, that states with large proportions of elderly persons having annual incomes under $3,000 have low out-migration rates of elderly persons. We conclude (but have no way of verifying it) that elderly persons with lower incomes are less likely to migrate than those with higher incomes. This type of problem is, of course, a shortcoming of most published research on migration. (But this observation does not reduce the importance of the difficulty.)

*Gross Flows*

State-of-origin to state-of-destination flows of *elderly* migrants are not known. The Census Bureau publishes the numbers of persons above five years of age moving from each state to each other state, but these figures are not disaggregated by age. We are constrained to use, therefore, gross and net migration figures for each state individually.

The importance of this limitation lies in the reduction in the types of information concerning causes which can be brought to bear on the migration statistics. For example, knowledge of the number of migrants from state A to state B would permit use of information about conditions in state A *and* in state B to explain this flow. But if only the number of persons who moved away from state A is known, then of course this flow away from state A cannot be explained with information concerning conditions in the destination areas. We only know the conditions in state A.

*Measurement Period*

Gross in-, gross out-, and net-migration figures for elderly persons are measured over a five-year period. That is, the data indicate how many people in the age group living in a given state in the census week of 1960 lived in another state in 1955. Likewise, the data indicate how many persons moved out of a given state between 1955 and the census week of 1960. These data allow net migration for each state to be computed over the period 1955 to 1960. The length of this period raises several difficulties.

**Cohort Selection**

First, because we must select an age-specific cohort based on age at the end of the migration period (1960), we cannot select a cohort which includes only persons aged 65 or greater *at the time they moved* without missing some of these older persons. The cohort must either include some persons who moved prior to age 65 or exclude some persons who moved after age 65. Table 3-1 will help explain this difficulty.

**Table 3-1**
**Alternative Age-Specific Cohorts**

| Cohort No. (Col. 1) | Minimum Age in 1955 (Col. 2) | Minimum Age in 1960 (Col. 3) | Persons Under Age 65 Included (Col. 4) | Persons Aged 65 and over Excluded (Col. 5) |
|---|---|---|---|---|
| 1 | 60 | 65 | 60-64 | – |
| 2 | 61 | 66 | 61-64 | 65 |
| 3 | 62 | 67 | 62-64 | 65-66 |
| 4 | 63 | 68 | 63-64 | 65-67 |
| 5 | 64 | 69 | 64 | 65-68 |
| 6 | 65 | 70 | – | 65-69 |

Columns 1 through 3 identify six different age-specific cohorts and their ages in both 1955 and 1960. Persons in the first cohort were at least age 60 in 1955 and at least age 65 in 1960; persons in the second at least age 61 in 1955 and at least age 66 in 1960; etc. Column 4 identifies the ages of persons included in each cohort who might have been under age 65 at the time they moved but who reached age 65 by 1960. The last column lists the ages of persons excluded from each cohort who could have been age 65 at the time they moved.

It is obvious that either some persons who moved prior to reaching age 65 must be included, or some persons who were 65 by 1960 must be excluded (or some combination of the two). For example, if we select the first cohort—persons at least 60 years old in 1955—those aged 60 through 64 are included, while none aged 65 or over is excluded. Selection of the third cohort excludes migration of persons aged 60 and 61 (included in the first cohort), but also excludes migration of persons who were ages 65 and 66 in 1960. The desired cohort—all persons who were 65 and over at the time they moved—cannot be achieved.

Based on discussions in Chapter 1 indicating that substantial retirement-oriented migration most probably occurs among persons under age 65, and given our interest in retirement migration, we have selected persons at least aged 65 in 1960 (cohort number 1 in the figure) for our prime study group. By doing this we miss as little "retirement migration" as possible.

## Excluded Migration

The second difficulty raised by the lengthy period of measurement of migration is the neglect of some kinds of complex, and possibly most interesting, movement. For example, if a family lived in state A in 1955, moved to state B in

1957, to state C in 1959, and back to state A in 1959, this movement does not register in the published statistics of migration. If the family moves to state D in 1959, rather than back to state A, this movement is registered in the statistics as movement of one family out of state A and the movement of one family into state D. The intervening movement is simply not recorded.

Also not recorded is seasonal migration of persons from, say, northern state A to southern state B in the winter and back again in the spring. If a couple began moving between states after 1955 and if during the census week they are in their "southern residence," they are counted as having moved once from state A to state B. If during the census week they are in their "northern residence," they are counted as having lived continuously in state A. In both cases the intervening moves are excluded. We suspect that there is a great deal of both kinds of migration (multiple state and seasonal), and it is unfortunate that we are not able to analyze it in this study.

**Dating Independent Variables**

A final problem encountered in any migration study, but magnified when the migration period is lengthened, arises because the correct time to measure the conditions which possibly influenced persons' decisions to move is not known. If annual migration statistics were available, conditions in each year could be compared with the numbers of persons leaving and entering each state in that year by assuming that conditions resulting in a move are contemporary with the move itself. But since it is not known very precisely when people moved (they may have moved any time between the census weeks in 1955 and 1960), some of the available information about the factors which influence migration must be discarded and averages computed covering several years.

*Statistical Errors*

Statistical information from any source contains errors. We have not investigated the nature or the extent of inaccuracy in all the data we have used relating to the independent variables. Errors in the migration statistics are especially interesting, however.

**Biased Response.** The Census Bureau reports that the 1960 census tended substantially to underestimate interstate mobility. Of persons classified as interstate migrants (between 1955 and 1960) in a post-census reinterview program, only 85.6 percent had been classified as interstate migrants in the census. Conversely, some persons were incorrectly classified as interstate migrants in the census. The net result of these two types of errors was that the number of interstate migrants reported in the census was only 92 percent of the number of persons so classified in the reinterview program.[3]

Furthermore, the bureau also reports that the crew leaders in the field during the enumeration in 1960 had an especially large effect on response variance for the 1955 residence questions. The response variance induced by crew leaders was larger in areas not highly urbanized than in highly urbanized areas.[4] This suggests that there might be some systemative variation among states in the accuracy of the migration figures.

**Sampling Error.** However accurate the field work may have been, the reported migration data are subject nevertheless to sampling error, since they are based on a 25 percent sample of the population. An illustration will suffice to demonstrate the magnitude of this problem. Wyoming experienced in-migration of elderly persons roughly equal to 6 percent of its 1960 population of elderly persons between 1955 and 1960. Given the size of this percentage and the population base, the Bureau of the Census reports that the standard error of this estimate is approximately .2. This means that the true value of the percentage of in-migration has a probability of .667 of lying between 5.8 and 6.2.[5]

Since Wyoming has a relatively small population, its standard error is relatively large. It is very unlikely, therefore, that for any *given* state the reported percentage differs substantially from the true percentage. But since the study is dealing with 48 states there is a fairly high probability of a few substantial errors. This possibility needs to be kept in mind when interpreting our statistical results.

*Selection Limitation*

The use of only published data has limited the types of independent variables that could be used in the analysis. For several of these variables, the readily available sources do not provide age breakdowns. For example, we have had to use the industrial structure of employment of all workers, rather than the industrial structure of employment of elderly workers. Similarly, wage incomes in various industries are available for all workers, but not for elderly workers alone. The median years of schooling of the adult population is readily available, but not the years of schooling of the elderly population. Finally, previous migration (1949-1950) of elderly persons, as a subgroup of all migrants, is not available.

**Statistical Techniques**

The third important limitation to the scope of our study lies in the technique of statistical analysis utilized. We have not been innovative in technique, but have used essentially the same methods of analysis that have been used by numerous other students of migration. In this section we first describe the elements of the methodology most often utilized in migration studies; then we briefly describe the minor differences between our procedures and those of other analysts; finally we describe the important shortcomings of this basic method.

*Normal Methodology*

The methodology usually employed can be broken down into several essential elements:

**Raw Data.** Data concerning migration to and from specified areas (usually states) are collected; likewise, data concerning the characteristics of these areas which are presumed to be relevant to the flows of population are also collected.

**Conversion to Rates.** The data on numbers of migrants are converted to migration rates. This is done by dividing the number of migrants to or from each state by the population of the relevant state. This operation has the effect of eliminating very large differences among states in the number of migrants, which presumably result from differences in base population. For example, the movement of a thousand persons out of North Dakota is made to seem larger than the movement of a thousand persons out of New York. Similarly, the measures of state characteristics which are thought to be relevant to migration flows are expressed in some sort of population-deflated form. For example, the number of persons unemployed is converted to the unemployment rate by dividing the number unemployed by the number of persons in the labor force.

**Multivariate Analysis.** It is assumed that the migration rates of the states are determined by the states' characteristics which have been measured:

$$M_i = M(X_{1,i}, X_{2,i}, X_{3,i}, \ldots, X_{n,i}),$$

where

$M_i$ is the migration of the $i$th state,

$X_{1,i}$ is the measure of the first relevant characteristic of the $i$th state,

$X_{2,i}$ is the measure of the second relevant characteristic of the $i$th state,

and so on.

Two forms of the function $M$ are frequently assumed: linear, and hyperbolic;

linear:

$$M_i = a_O + a_1 X_{1,i} + a_2 X_{2,i} + \ldots + a_n X_{n,i} + u_i$$

and hyperbolic:

$$M_i = b_O X_{1,i}^{b_1} X_{2,i}^{b_2} X_{3,i}^{b_3} \ldots X_{n,i}^{bn} e_i$$

where the $a_O - a_n$ and $b_O - b_n$ are constant parameters, and the $u_i$ and $e_i$ are errors or random variations of the $i$th state's migration rate.

The hyperbolic form has the advantage that the parameters, $b_j$, can be interpreted as elasticities. That is, they tell us the predicted percentage difference in $M$ caused by a one percent difference in any $X_j$. These elasticities are constant; that is, they do not depend on the reference values of $M$ and $X$. A related advantage of the hyperbolic form is that the $b$'s can be directly compared with each other, while the $a$'s from the linear functional form cannot be directly compared. The reason for this difference in the interpretation of the coefficients is that the sizes of the $a$'s depend on the units in which the $X$'s are measured, whereas the $b$'s have no such dependence.

The parameters of either the linear or the hyperbolic function are estimated by the least-squares fitting technique. In the case of the hyperbolic form, this technique is applied to the natural logarithms of $M_i$ and $X_{j,i}$.

*Differences in Present Methodology*

Since we focus on migration of elderly persons, we define the $M$'s (migration rates) in which we are most interested, and as many as possible of our $X$'s (independent variables), with this more special focus in view. The majority of the migration rates studied in this book are the numbers of persons moving into (or out of, or the difference between in-movement and out-movement) each state, whose age in 1960 was 65 or greater or whose age was between 65 and 69 inclusive. Where available data have permitted, independent variables are included, which should be especially relevant to elderly persons. For example, in addition to unemployment rates for the total labor force (which are frequently used as independent variables in studies of migration of the population as a whole), unemployment rates of elderly persons also are utilized.

**Elderly versus Young.** We have also explored the differences between migration rates for elderly persons and for non-elderly persons (those under age 65 in 1960). Our intention here is to see if the variables which are not age-specific in their expected influence on migration affect elderly persons in a substantially different manner than they influence younger persons.

**Multiple Hypotheses.** Most investigators of migration patterns set out to test one or two simple hypotheses. Consequently, they utilize relatively few independent variables ($X$'s). In contrast, we have enumerated (in Chapter 1) several hypotheses. These hypotheses are represented in our statistical analysis by 63 independent variables. We allow the data to dictate which variable or variables best measure the characteristics of states suggested by our hypotheses, and to indicate the relative strength of our hypotheses in accounting for the observed pattern of migration rates.

*Statistical Difficulties*

There are several important difficulties encountered in using the procedure outlined in the above two sections: separating the "causes" from the "effects," and multicollinearity in the independent variables.

**Cause and Effect.** Regression analysis allows us to measure the statistical association between the variables to be explained ($M$'s) and the explanatory variables ($X$'s). The finding of statistical association does not, however, demonstrate that variation in the $X$'s causes variation in the $M$'s. It could very well be the other way around. For example, we hypothesize that states with high unemployment rates of elderly persons will have high out-migration of elderly persons and low in-migration. Suppose, however, that elderly migrants frequently remain unemployed after their movement, so that large in-migration rates result in high unemployment rates. This might lead to positive association between unemployment rates and in-migration rates, contrary to the original hypothesis. It then is difficult to interpret the positive association between unemployment rates and in-migration rates. This finding may show that the hypothesis is not correct, or it might simply show that the other effect (elderly persons remaining unemployed following a move) dominates the hypothesized effect in the data and renders it invisible. Such mutual, or circular, causation situations are frequently encountered in empirical research in economics, and a body of method has been developed to deal with them statistically. These methods, however, have not been widely employed with cross-sectional data.

**Multicollinearity.** The explanatory variables are correlated not only with the variables to be explained, but also with each other. This multicollinearity makes it difficult to separate the influences of the independent variables. Furthermore, the values of the coefficients ($a$'s or $b$'s) are biased when variables which are highly correlated with each other are used to explain another variable. No recognized, established procedures have been developed for dealing with this problem. When possible, we point out instances in which multicollinearity is exceptionally strong.

# 30

## Definition of Migration Variables

We calculate 30 different migration rates; 21 of these rates relate to persons aged 65 or over, 9 relate to persons aged 64 or less. Tables 3-2 and 3-3 describe these

**Table 3-2**
**Description of Type of Migration, Sex, and Age, by Migration Variable**

| Variable | Type of Migration | | | Sex Category | | | Age Category | | | |
|---|---|---|---|---|---|---|---|---|---|---|
| | In | Out | Net | Male | Female | All | 65+ | 65-69 | 70+ | 64- |
| $M_1$ | X | | | X | | | X | | | |
| $M_2$ | X | | | | X | | X | | | |
| $M_3$ | X | | | | | X | X | | | |
| $M_4$ | | X | | X | | | X | | | |
| $M_5$ | | X | | | X | | X | | | |
| $M_6$ | | X | | | | X | X | | | |
| $M_7$ | | | X | | | | X | | | |
| $M_8$ | | | X | | X | | X | | | |
| $M_9$ | | | X | | | X | X | | | |
| $M_{10}$ | X | | | X | | | | X | | |
| $M_{11}$ | X | | | | X | | | X | | |
| $M_{12}$ | X | | | | | X | | X | | |
| $M_{13}$ | | X | | X | | | | X | | |
| $M_{14}$ | | X | | | X | | | X | | |
| $M_{15}$ | | X | | | | X | | X | | |
| $M_{16}$ | | | X | X | | | | X | | |
| $M_{17}$ | | | X | | X | | | X | | |
| $M_{18}$ | | | X | | | X | | X | | |
| $M_{19}$ | | | X | X | | | | | X | |
| $M_{20}$ | | | X | | X | | | | X | |
| $M_{21}$ | | | X | | | X | | | X | |
| $M_{22}$ | X | | | X | | | | | | X |
| $M_{23}$ | X | | | | X | | | | | X |
| $M_{24}$ | X | | | | | X | | | | X |
| $M_{25}$ | | X | | X | | | | | | X |
| $M_{26}$ | | X | | | X | | | | | X |
| $M_{27}$ | | X | | | | X | | | | X |
| $M_{28}$ | | | X | X | | | | | | X |
| $M_{29}$ | | | X | | X | | | | | X |
| $M_{30}$ | | | X | | | X | | | | X |

**Table 3-3**
**Migration Variables Categorized by Age, Sex, and Type of Migration**

| Age Group | Gross In | | | Gross Out | | | Net (In-Out) | | |
|---|---|---|---|---|---|---|---|---|---|
| | Male | Female | All | Male | Female | All | Male | Female | All |
| 65+ | $M_1$ | $M_2$ | $M_3$ | $M_4$ | $M_5$ | $M_6$ | $M_7$ | $M_8$ | $M_9$ |
| 65-69 | $M_{10}$ | $M_{11}$ | $M_{12}$ | $M_{13}$ | $M_{14}$ | $M_{15}$ | $M_{16}$ | $M_{17}$ | $M_{18}$ |
| 70+ | | | | | | | $M_{19}$ | $M_{20}$ | $M_{21}$ |
| 64- | $M_{22}$ | $M_{23}$ | $M_{24}$ | $M_{25}$ | $M_{26}$ | $M_{27}$ | $M_{28}$ | $M_{29}$ | $M_{30}$ |

Type of Migration

migration rates (used as dependent variables–*M*'s in later discussions) utilized in this book. Table 3-2 allows the reader to find the definition of any particular variable by locating the label ($M_i$) of the variable and reading across to find the type of migration, sex category, and age category for that variable. Table 3-3 allows the reader to find the label of any dependent variable by locating the appropriate age-sex-type of migration cell in the matrix.

For every variable the denominator of the migration rate is the appropriate age-sex-population of each state for 1960. The numerators are, of course, the number of in- or out-migrants of the difference between these numbers in any given age-sex category for the period 1955-1960.[a] Variables $M_{19}$, $M_{20}$, and $M_{21}$, relating to net migration rates for persons aged 70 and over, are for the period 1950-1960 due to data limitations.

## *Use of Gross Rates*

Our discussions concentrate on gross migration rates. There are three reasons for our relative neglect of net migration rates. First since net migration rates are just differences between gross migration rates, understanding of influences on net rates requires understanding of gross rates, while the obverse is not true. That is, any observed influence on a net migration rate must result from an influence on the corresponding in-migration rate or on the corresponding out-migration rate, or on both.

Second, net migration rates do not lend themselves to analysis in terms of constant elasticity relationships. This is because logarithms of negative net migration rates do not exist. We have adopted the simple expedient of defining

[a]As indicated elsewhere the logarithms of all variables are utilized rather than their absolute values in all correlation and regression analysis. This necessitated adding "one" to any of the migration rates with potential negative or zero values. Since gross migration rates are always positive, only net migration rates were so adjusted prior to taking the logs. These variables are $M_7$ - $M_9$, $M_{16}$ - $M_{21}$, and $M_{28}$ - $M_{30}$.

our variables as net migration rates plus unity. Consequently, interpretation of the net migration results is not parallel to that for gross migration rates.

Third, we find much more striking relationships between gross migration rates and the independent variables than between the independent variables and net migration rates. It could be argued, and pursuasively, that net migration rates are more important in policy discussions than are gross migration rates. However, since the goal of this book is not to provide specific answers to any *particular* policy questions, but rather to begin building scientific understanding of elderly migration patterns, we feel the emphasis on gross migration rates is amply justified.

*Some Observations*

Our purpose here is not to describe in great detail migration patterns of older persons, but rather to point out some interesting aspects of those patterns and changes in those patterns as estimated through census data. In several notable instances, migration patterns of the older population diverge from those of younger persons in ways which cannot be explained by casual observation; multivariate analysis offers a potential for better understanding of such differences.

**Low Migration Rates.** A brief examination of selected migration rates reveals several interesting aspects of elderly persons' (those aged 65 and over) migration patterns relative to those of younger persons (those aged 64 and under). First, and already noted in Chapter 1, is the lower mobility rates of the elderly relative to younger population groups. As Table 3-4 indicates, gross migration rates of younger persons are more than double those of older persons in both the 1955-1960 and 1965-1970 periods.

**Movement into Small States.** Second, there is a general movement of elderly persons away from larger states toward smaller states. This in itself is not remarkable, but this movement is the *reverse* of that noted for younger persons, who are moving away from smaller, toward larger states. This overall movement of the elderly toward smaller states can be seen by examining the mean net migration rates contained in Table 3-4. Since a given size population movement results in higher *rates* of movement in smaller than in larger states, a net movement into smaller states will result in a positive value for the mean of all states' net migration rates. A reverse movement will yield a negative mean for net rates.

The net migration rates for persons aged 65 and over in the two periods 1955-1960 and 1965-1970 are .0015 and .003 respectively; those for younger

**Table 3-4**
**Means, Standard Deviations, and Coefficients of Variation for Selected Migration Rates**

| Migration Rate | Mean $(\overline{X})$ | | Standard Deviation $(\sigma)$ | | Coefficient of Variation $\dfrac{\sigma}{\overline{X}}(100)$ | |
|---|---|---|---|---|---|---|
| | 1955-1960 | 1965-1970 | 1955-1960 | 1965-1970 | 1955-1960 | 1965-1970 |
| Persons Aged 65+ | | | | | | |
| Gross In-Mig. | .04604 | .04585 | .04772 | .03410 | 103.7 | 77.9 |
| Gross Out-Mig. | .04464 | .04302 | .01731 | .01685 | 38.8 | 39.2 |
| Net Mig. | .00147 | .00262 | .04469 | nc | nc | nc |
| Persons Aged 65-69 | | | | | | |
| Gross In-Mig. | .07561 | .05131 | .12619 | .04981 | 166.4 | 97.1 |
| Gross Out-Mig. | .04950 | .04750 | .02139 | .02099 | 43.2 | 44.2 |
| Net Mig. | .00228 | .00385 | .05642 | nc | nc | nc |
| Persons Aged 64- | | | | | | |
| Gross In-Mig. | .10013 | .10656 | .05306 | .04139 | 53.0 | 38.8 |
| Gross Out-Mig. | .10442 | .11054 | .03476 | .03919 | 33.3 | 35.5 |
| Net Mig. | −.00414 | −.00296 | .04301 | nc | nc | nc |

nc−not calculated.

persons are −.004 and −.003.[b] The movement toward smaller states by older persons is even more evident among the subgroups of persons aged 65 to 69, for which the respective means in the two periods are .002 and .004. Of interest here is the fact that the means of the net migration rates of both older groups moved further away from zero in the second period, suggesting an intensification in the relative movement *away* from large states by older persons. Additionally, even though gross migration rates of younger persons increased between the the two decades, the net migration rate of the group fell; at the same time, net migration rates of both groups of older persons rose—that of persons aged 65-69 to a level exceeding (the absolute level of) that of younger persons.

[b]It should be pointed out that only if the following conditions were met would the means for gross in- and gross out-migration rates for any one population group be equal, or net migration rates be zero: (1) zero net movement into or out of the 48 continental states; (2) migrants and non-migrants in each state having the same relative death rates; and (3) all movements taking place between states with population groups of equal size. Since these conditions clearly are not met, gross in- and gross out-migration rates are not equal, nor are net migration rates zero. The first two factors above involve relatively small numbers of persons, so it is thought that most of the explanation for non-zero net migration rates lies in movements between states of unequal size.

**"Modal Direction" in Migration.** Third, elderly persons show a greater tendency to move into a few specific states than do younger persons. While migration rates for the younger population group exceeds those for the older group, a glance of the last two columns of Table 3-4 reveals that the variation in the in-migration rates of elderly persons for specific states (as measured by coefficients of variation) exceeds that for younger persons. The coefficients of variation is larger yet for the elderly group aged 65 through 69. Over the period 1955-1960, this statistic for the young, the elderly, and persons aged 65 through 69, respectively, is 53.0, 103.7, and 166.4. This extreme variation in the in-migration rates of both older groups decreased in the later period, but was still more than double that associated with persons aged 64 and under.

These differences in intensity of a "modal direction" in migration can be seen more clearly in Figure 3-1. Gross in-migration rates over the period 1955-1960 are measured on the vertical axis, and the seven highest in-migration rates by state are ranked on the horizontal axis for each of the three population groups. Persons aged 65-69 had the highest in-migration rates to specific states, with movements into three states equalling or exceeding the highest rates of the other two groups, but falling off very rapidly in successive states. While rates for persons under age 65 all exceed those for persons aged 65 and over (when ranked in descending order), successive migration rates for the younger group decrease relatively slowly. Such differences were maintained for the period 1965-1970, but the differences are not so accentuated.

In no state does the 1965-1970 gross out-migration rate of persons aged 65 and over exceed that of persons aged 64 and under, and in only one state (Florida) does the gross in-migration rate of older persons exceed that of younger persons. On the other hand, the *net* migration rates of persons aged 65 and over *exceed those of persons under age 65 in 15 states.* In seven of the states, net out-migration is higher, and in eight states, net in-migration is higher. These states are contained in Table 3-5. This implies that the impact on individual states' economies of migration patterns of older persons is more substantial than the relative gross migration rates of older versus younger persons suggests.

**High Out-Migration.** Finally, some surprising states show up with high out-migration rates of elderly persons. Table 3-6 contains a list of the eight states with the highest 1955-1960 out-migration rates of older persons, and those states' rates in the period 1965-1970. All eight states are western states, with five of them being no surprise. However, the appearance of Nevada (.106), New Mexico (.072), and Arizona (.063), all states with extremely high in-migration rates of elderly persons, is unexpected. Not only were the out-migration rates from those states high in the second half of the 1950s, they were even higher in each of these three states in the later period. At the same time, out-migration rates from the other five states in the list were falling.

**Table 3-5**

**States in Which 1965-1970 Net Migration Rates of Persons Aged 65 and Over Exceed those of Persons Aged 64 and Under**

| Higher Net Out-Migration | Higher Net In-Migration |
|---|---|
| Illinois | Arizona |
| Indiana | Florida |
| Massachusetts | Nevada |
| Minnesota | North Carolina |
| New York | Oklahoma |
| Ohio | Oregon |
| Wisconsin | South Carolina |
| | Tennessee |

Source: U.S. Department of Commerce, Bureau of the Census, *U.S. Census of Population, 1970: Subject Reports, Mobility for States and the Nation*, Final Report PC(2)-2B (Washington, D.C.: Government Printing Office, 1973), Table 59.

**Geographic Trends in the 1960s.** Looking at broad regions of the United States, it can be seen that migration of older persons is resulting in their redistribution away from the New England, Middle Atlantic, and East North Central groups of states toward other regions, and that this exodus is most rapid from the Middle Atlantic states (Table 3-7).

A more revealing picture of the changing distribution of older persons can be seen in Figure 3-2. It identifies those states whose elderly population grew at a more rapid rate than that of the U.S. total. Only states in the southern half of the United States, or on one of the seaboards, were increasing their populations of older persons more rapidly than the U.S. average. Mississippi is the only such state which did not. Clearly, older persons have definite geographic preferences.

In all, 29 states showed positive net migration of older persons during the 1960s, but a relatively few of them received the majority of in-migrants. Six states alone (all in the southern or coastal states identified in Figure 3-2) accounted for 80.2 percent of the population gains through migration. They are identified in Table 3-8. Of course, the relative impact of these population gains through migration are not directly proportionate to the numbers of such migrants. The 142,000 net migrants to California probably had less relative impact on the state than the 46,000 net migrants to Arizona. Migration of older persons into Florida accounted for 84 percent of that state's gain in over-64 population (366,000 of 436,000) in this ten-year period. Arizona followed at 65 percent, with Oregon's 40.5 percent third. The 142,000 gain attributable to migration in California contributed 33.6 percent to that state's gain in elderly population. It is in these states (identified in Table 3-8) that migration of older persons has the greatest significance.

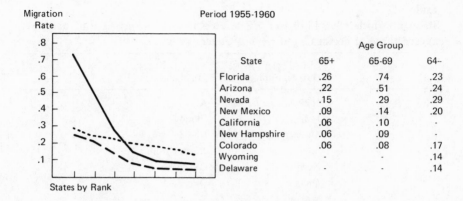

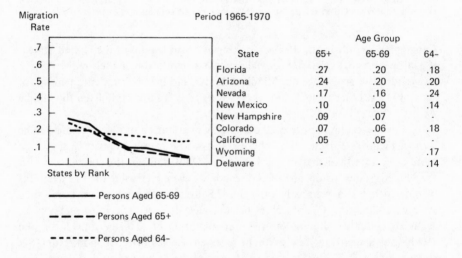

**Figure 3-1**. In-Migration Rates for Selected States, 1955-1960, and 1965-1970.


## Comments and Caveats

In the chapters which follow we discuss both correlation coefficients between the logarithms of the migration rates and the logarithms of the independent variables and multiple regression coefficients. We believe that the correlation results are generally more meaningful, and we therefore emphasize them in the exposition. There are two reasons for this belief.

**Table 3-6**

**Gross Out-Migration Rates of Persons Aged 65+ for Selected States, 1955-1960 and 1965-1970**

| State | Migration Rate | |
|---|---|---|
| | 1955-1960 | 1965-1970 |
| Nevada | .106 | .109 |
| Wyoming | .090 | .075 |
| New Mexico | .072 | .075 |
| South Dakota | .072 | .045 |
| Idaho | .065 | .053 |
| Arizona | .063 | .077 |
| North Dakota | .063 | .060 |
| Montana | .061 | .059 |

Source: U.S. Department of Commerce, Bureau of the Census, *U.S. Census of Population, 1960: Subject Reports, Mobility for States and State Economic Areas*, Final Report PC(2)-2B (Washington, D.C.: Government Printing Office, 1962), Table 24. U.S. Department of Commerce, Bureau of the Census, *U.S. Census of Population, 1970: Subject Reports, Mobility for States and the Nation*, Final Report PC(2)-2B (Washington, D.C.: Government Printing Office, 1973), Table 59.

First, the sheer number of independent variables used means that in any given multiple regression equation, only a small proportion of them can be entered before the partial correlation coefficients of the remaining variables become statistically insignificant. The result is that, except for a few variables which appear in several equations, the collections of variables in the equations give the appearance of having been randomly selected.

**Table 3-7**

**Net Migration Rates of Persons Aged 65 and Over, by Geographic Region, 1960-1970**

| Positive In-Migration Regions | | Negative In-Migration Regions | |
|---|---|---|---|
| Region | Rate | Region | Rate |
| South Atlantic | 8.4 | Middle Atlantic | −4.5 |
| Mountain | 6.5 | East North Central | −3.5 |
| Pacific | 4.6 | New England | −1.4 |
| West South Central | 2.9 | | |
| East South Central | 0.7 | | |
| West North Central | 0.3 | | |

Source: U.S., Bureau of the Census, *Current Population Reports*, Series P-23 No. 43, "Some Demographic Aspects of Aging in the United States" (Washington, D.C.: U.S. Government Printing Office, 1973), Table 9, p. 11.

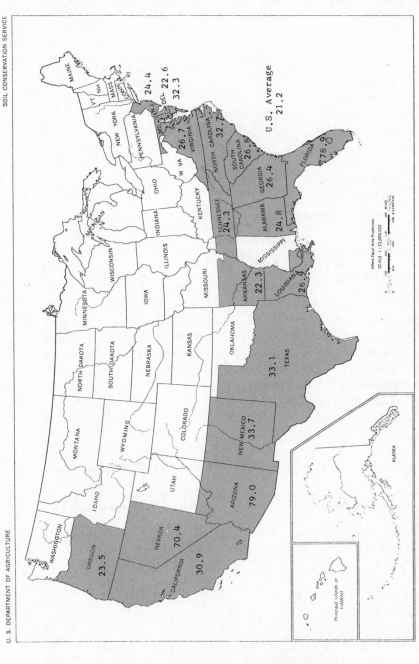

**Figure 3-2.** States Having Faster than Average Growth Rates of Elderly Population, 1960-1970. Source: U.S. Bureau of the Census, *Current Population Reports*, Series P-23, No. 43, "Some Demographic Aspects of Aging in the United States," (Washington, D.C.: U.S. Government Printing Office, 1973), Table 8, p. 10.

**Table 3-8**
**States with Largest Increases in Elderly Attributable to Migration**

| State | Population Gain Through Net Migration | Proportion of Gain Attributable to Migration |
|---|---|---|
| Florida | 366,122 | .840 |
| Arkansas | 17,750 | .403 |
| Texas | 52,762 | .214 |
| Arizona | 46,176 | .650 |
| Oregon | 17,176 | .405 |
| California | 142,886 | .336 |
| Six-State Total | 643,109 | |

Source: U.S., Bureau of the Census, *Current Population Reports*, Series P-23 No. 43, "Some Demographic Aspects of Aging in the United States" (Washington, D.C.: U.S. Government Printing Office, 1973), Table 9, p. 11.

Second, the correlation coefficients suggest to us that many of our variables are influenced by migration more than they influence migrations. When we consider the correlation coefficients only, we feel that we can frequently infer interesting conclusions about migration patterns. But inclusion of such variables in multiple regressions violates the fundamental assumptions of that technique. Not only are the regression coefficients of these variables suspect, but the coefficients of other variables in the equation are also subject to biases in estimation. In other words, statistical problems with one or a few variables contaminate the *entire* regression equation in which they appear. This type of contamination is present though not usually emphasized in almost all statistical studies of determinants of migration.

**Summary and Conclusions**

Since this book represents an exploratory effort designed to suggest the nature of the influences acting on migration of elderly persons, restrictions are imposed as to the scope and methodology of our research. Our investigation is limited to interstate migration, and we utilize readily available, published data. These restrictions prevent the use of some possibly important variables and place limits on the population movements we can examine. But given the absence of previous work on which to build, our interest is to examine a large number of potential influences on migration of the elderly, identifying the more important variables, and raising specific questions for more detailed research in the future. For these tasks, we hope that our research approach is appropriate.

## Notes

1. U.S. Department of Commerce, Bureau of the Census, *1960 Census of Population, Special Reports, Mobility of States and State Economic Areas*, Final Report (Washington, D.C.: U.S. Government Printing Office, 1962), Table 3.

2. Ibid.

3. Ibid., p. xiv.

4. U.S. Department of Commerce, Bureau of the Census, Evaluation and Research Program of the U.S. Censuses of Population and Housing, 1960: *Effects of Interviewers and Crew Leaders*, Series ER60, No. 7 (Washington, D.C.: U.S. Government Printing Office, 1968), pp. 40-43.

5. U.S. Census, *Mobility of States*, p. xxi.

# 4 Influence of Past Migration

Other students of migration have noted a high relationship between the direction and magnitude of population movements in one period and movements in some subsequent period.[1] None of these studies, however, has been concerned with elderly persons. Since the relationship between current and past population movements may be quite complex, the first section of this chapter explores the various ways in which past migration might influence current migration. The second tests the relationship between migration from 1955 to 1960 as it is related to earlier migration.

We find that data limitations of this study do not permit us to test alternative ways in which migration in different periods might be related. We *are* able to test for the existence of the relationship, however, and find that not only are interstate movements of elderly persons between 1955 and 1960 closely related to previous population movements, but that earlier migration patterns appear to offer one of the more important explanations of later migration. This also is true for younger persons.

## Association Between Past and Current Migration Rates

Three possible explanations as to why migration rates into or out of any given area should be sequentially related offer themselves:

1. the flow of information from actual migrants to potential migrants;
2. the attractiveness of areas where friends and relatives of potential migrants are located; and
3. the relatively slow rates of change in factors affecting migration patterns.

We will examine these explanations in order.

### Flow of Information

Imagine a closed region (no movement across the boundaries) divided into three subregions—Region A, Region B, and Region C. Suppose that in an initial period—Period 0—the population is in locational equilibrium in the limited sense

41

that each family, *as far as it knows*, lives in its optimal region. Some families actually do live in their optimal regions; others could find greater satisfaction in other locations, but they do not know it. In such a situation there will be no migration.

In Period 1, families begin to receive information about conditions—employment opportunities, climate, health and educational facilities, etc.—in other regions. This information, however, is not generally believed to be absolutely reliable. There will now be some migration. Families which move will have two characteristics: they will find that, based on the available information, there is some better region than that in which they are currently living; and they will have a relatively low aversion to risk. This latter characteristic is required because migration is a risky enterprise where the information on which it is based is of dubious quality, as assumed here.

Now further assume that the information available in Period 1 was generally correct, so that most of those who moved in the period find that they are better satisfied in their new locations than they were in their old locations. In Period 2 these migrants will be communicating with their friends and relatives in their prior locations. The information they will be conveying about their new locations will be essentially the same as that which was available in the first period. Some families which did not move in Period 1 have now received the same information twice, but the second time from sources which they consider more reliable than in the first period, since they have heard it from people they know. Thus in Period 2, there will be further migration. The new migrants will be families who find, based on the new information, that there are better places to live than those in which they are currently living. These families will differ from those who moved in Period 1 in that their aversion to risk is greater; they were only induced to move when information they subjectively regarded as reliable became available, even though the substance of the information was unchanged.

How will the number of migrants out of (into) each region in Periods 1 and 2 be related? Let us define as "potential migrants" all those families which could actually achieve greater satisfaction in regions other than their current locations. "Actual migrants" are initially potential migrants, but become actual migrants after movement. Suppose the number of potential migrants at the beginning of Period 1 is the same in each region, but that the number who become actual migrants is larger in Region A than in Regions B and C (because, for some reason, there are more families with low aversion to risk in Region A). Also assume that in Region A the number of actual migrants in Period 1 is a small percentage of the number of potential migrants at the beginning of the period. In Period 2 some families in each region will be receiving information about other regions from the actual migrants of Period 1. But since most families in each region do not know any of the migrants of the previous period, most families are not receiving any information. It is clear, however, that the number

of families in Region A receiving information from this source is greater than the number receiving information in Regions B and C. And, since this information tends to produce more migration in Period 2, more families will move away from Region A in Period 2 than from Regions B and C. There will be, therefore, positive correlation between the out-migration rates in Periods 1 and 2.

Suppose the number of actual migrants (Period 2) into Region B is larger than the number of migrants into Regions A and C. The migrants in each region are sending information back to their friends and relatives in their original locations concerning conditions in the new regions. Since in each region more families are receiving information about Region B than about Regions A and C, the number of potential migrants who actually move to Region B will be larger than the number who move to Regions A and C. Therefore, there will be positive correlation between in-migration rates in Periods 1 and 2.

## Influence of Friends and Relatives

The above argument simply states that potential migrants will become actual migrants when the flow of reliable information reduces adequately the risk of migration. Our second argument is that migration into a region in one period will make that region more attractive, increase the number of potential migrants and, therefore, increase the number of actual migrants. The reason is that migrants not only convey information to their friends and relatives "back home" about objective conditions in their new locations, but they also, by their presence in the new locations, change the objective conditions. Suppose, for example, that there is a family in locational equilibrium living in Region A in Period 0, and that the information available in Period 1, even if the family regards it as absolutely reliable, does not cause the family to wish to move. However, another family, close friends of the first family, does move in Period 1 to, say, Region B. Now, the presence of this family in Region B may make Region B sufficiently attractive to cause the first family to move from Region A to Region B.

If this phenomenon is fairly common, one should expect migration rates in Periods 1 and 2 to be positively correlated. Regions which experience high rates of out-migration in Period 1 will also experience high out-migration rates in Period 2, since many families now have friends or relatives in other regions. Likewise, regions which experience high rates of in-migration in Period 1 should experience high rates in Period 2 for the same reason.

## Stability of Conditions

These first two reasons for sequential association of migration rates are based on assumptions about human behavior. These assumptions result in the propositions

that high migration rates in one period *cause* high migration rates in later periods, and that low migration rates in one period *cause* low migration rates in later periods. The argument we will now present is of a different kind. We will show that under certain plausible conditions migration rates will be sequentially correlated, even though there is no direct causal link between migration rates in one period and rates in a later period.

Suppose for simplicity that the arguments we have already presented are not valid—that potential migrants do not depend on friends and relatives in other regions for information about those regions, and that families do not regard the locations of friends and relatives as relevant information in making locational choices. The rate of migration in Period 1 is then based solely on objective conditions in the various regions—employment opportunities, geography, weather, etc. All potential migrants actually move. Now assume that the objective conditions which are relevant to locational choices remain the same in Period 2. During the period the pool of potential migrants in each region is replenished through natural increase and aging of the population (various families reach ages at which migration is most likely). In Period 2 the pattern of migration will be very similar to that of Period 1, because the objective conditions affecting the relative attractiveness of the regions are unchanged. Therefore, positive correlation would be observed between in-migration rates in Periods 1 and 2 and between out-migration rates in Periods 1 and 2. But one could not conclude that high (low) migration rates in Period 1 *caused* high (low) migration rates in Period 2.

**Statistical Results**

If the only reason for sequential association of migration rates were the stability of conditions discussed above, there would be no need to use previous migration rates as explanatory variables for current migration rates. In fact, the results would be misleading. Previous migration rates would be standing in on the right side of the regression equations as proxies for the things (some of which are certainly unknown) which caused migration in the prior period, which are probably the same things causing migration in the current period. However, the first two arguments for sequential association discussed in Section 1 require taking account of previous migration in our statistical analysis, since they suggest that prior migration rates have direct causative influence on current migration rates. We have, therefore (with some misgivings), used previous migration rates to explain current migration rates.

*Description of Independent Variables*

Unfortunately, the 1950 census data on migration are much less complete than those from the 1960 census. They cover only a one-year period—1949-

1950—and they are not disaggregated by age. The latter flaw is probably the more serious. If we knew 1949-1950 migration rates by age group we could discover, possibly, whether 1955-1960 migration rates of elderly persons are more closely associated with earlier migration rates of persons of roughly the same age, or with rates for persons much younger, or with the rates for persons for all ages. As it is, we can only measure the association of 1955-1960 migration rates of elderly persons with 1949-1950 migration rates of the population aged five years and older. (Sex disaggregation of the earlier figures are available, but we have not used this additional information.) These migration rates are defined as follows:

$X_1$ = Number of in-migrants aged five years and older, 1949-1950 divided by 1950 population aged five years and older

$X_2$ = Number of out-migrants aged five years and older, 1949-1950 divided by 1950 population aged five years and older

$X_3$ = Number of in-migrants minus number of out-migrants $(X_1 - X_2)$ divided by 1950 population

In-, out-, and net migration among the states between 1949 and 1950 are highly intercorrelated. The simple correlations between the logarithms of these three migration variables are as follows:

$$r_{X_1 X_2} = .949, r_{X_1 X_3} = .584, \text{ and } r_{X_2 X_3} = .329.$$

These correlations indicate that states with the highest gross in-migration rates between 1949 and 1950 also had the highest gross out-migration rates, and that the association between these migration rates is very regular. Gross in- and gross out-migration rates are less closely associated with net migration rates than they are with each other, but all these correlations are significant at the .01 level of significance.[a]

*States with High and Low Migration Rates*

Table 4-1 identifies the states with the highest and lowest 1949-1950 gross in- and gross out-migration rates, and those with the highest positive net and highest negative net migration rates. Even knowing of the extremely high simple correlation between gross in- and gross out-migration, we were surprised to find that the four states with the highest gross in-migration rates were also those with

[a]The reader is again reminded that in this book all correlation and regression results refer to the logarithms of the variables. In a few cases (notably net migration) the variables are the logarithms of the original variable, plus unity. On the other hand, references to the means, standard deviations, or coefficients of variation, relate to the raw data.

**Table 4-1**

**Gross In-, Gross Out-, and Net-Migration Rates for Selected States, 1949-1950**

High Migration Rates

| Gross In-Mig. | | Gross Out-Mig. | | High Positive Net Migration | |
|---|---|---|---|---|---|
| State | Rate | State | Rate | State | Rate |
| Nevada | .101 | Nevada | .095 | Florida | .021 |
| Wyoming | .082 | Wyoming | .081 | Maryland | .013 |
| New Mexico | .077 | Arizona | .073 | New Mexico | .016 |
| Arizona | .075 | New Mexico | .061 | Texas | .009 |

Low Migration Rates

| Gross In-Mig. | | Gross Out-Mig. | | High Negative Net Migration | |
|---|---|---|---|---|---|
| State | Rate | State | Rate | State | Rate |
| New York | .010 | Penn. | .014 | N.H. | −.010 |
| Penn. | .010 | Michigan | .016 | Maine | −.009 |
| Mass. | .014 | Mass. | .017 | Arkansas | −.009 |
| Maine | .015 | N. Carolina | .017 | N. Dakota | −.007 |

Source: U.S., Department of Commerce, Bureau of the Census, *U.S. Census of Population, 1950*, Vol. II, *Characteristics of Population* (Washington, D.C.: Government Printing Office, 1950), Table 9.

the highest gross out-migration rates (cols. 1 and 2). Nevada experienced the highest gross in- and highest gross out-migration rates (.101 and .095 respectively) of all states. Wyoming, New Mexico, and Arizona follow. Two of the four states with the lowest in-migration rates—Pennsylvania and Massachusetts—also were in the group with the lowest out-migration rates.

Because of the close association between gross population movements only one of the four states with the highest gross in-migration rates between 1949 and 1950—New Mexico—also was in the group of four with the highest (positive) net migration rates. None of the four states with the highest gross out-migration rates was in the group with the largest net population losses from migration. Florida (.021), Maryland (.013), New Mexico (.016), and Texas (.009) gained most from population movements. New Hampshire (.010), Maine (.009), Arkansas, (.009) and North Dakota (.007) lost population at the highest rates.

*Simple Correlation Coefficients*

Simple correlations between previous migration variables ($X_1$, $X_2$, and $X_3$) and subsequent migration rates for elderly persons between 1955 and 1960 are contained in Table 4-2. Whatever the underlying chain of causation, it is clear from the correlations in Table 4-2 that there is a strong sequential association of migration rates. This sequential association is strongest for in-migration rates and weakest for net migration rates. Each of the current migration rates is correlated with three past migration rates (gross in- and gross out-migration, and net migration). For each of these current rates, the highest correlation is with the corresponding past rate; i.e., current in-migration is more closely associated with past in-migration (.783) than with either past out- or past net migration, and similar relationships hold between current out- and past out-migration and between current net- and past net-migration.

One way of interpreting the ranking of the sequential correlations is as follows: in-migration rates in individual states changed less between 1949-1950 and 1955-1960 than did out-migration rates, which changed less than net migration rates. In other words, states with characteristics which attracted relatively large numbers of in-migrants in 1949-1950 continued to do so between 1955 and 1960, but in-migrants' states of origin tended to change between the two periods.

**Stability of Migration Patterns.** Interpreting the simple correlations as indicators of relative stability of migration patterns permits another observation. These

**Table 4-2**
**Simple Correlation Coefficients Between Migration Rates in 1949-1950 and 1955-1960[a]**

| Migration Rates | $X_1$ | $X_2$ | $X_3$ |
|---|---|---|---|
| Gross In-Migration | | | |
| All Persons Aged 65+ | .783* | .724 | .528* |
| Gross Out-Migration | | | |
| All Persons Aged 65+ | .518 | .632* | .039 |
| Net Migration | | | |
| All Persons Aged 65+ | .443* | .344 | .568* |
| Gross In-Migration | | | |
| All Persons Aged 64- | .921* | .877 | .569* |
| Gross Out-Migration | | | |
| All Persons Aged 64- | .736 | .838* | .083 |
| Net Migration | | | |
| All Persons Aged 64- | .465* | .342 | .631* |

[a]Coefficients with expected signs are identified by an asterisk (*); those significant at the .05 level of confidence by a single underscore, and those significant at the .01 level of significance by a double underscore.

correlations for each of the three migration variables in Table 4-2 are higher for younger persons than for older persons. The corresponding gross in-, gross out-, and net migration correlations for the two groups respectively are .921 versus .783 (for "in"), .838 versus .632 (for "out") and .631 versus .568 (for "net"). The smaller correlations for each of the migration variables for older persons suggest that they changed their migration patterns between the two periods to a greater extent than did younger persons. The explanation for this is unknown, although several possibilities exist. Increases in incomes of older persons between the periods could have allowed them to exercise their locational choice to a greater extent than was possible earlier, so that even though the desired retirement locations did not change, the ability to move to them did. It also is possible that changes were occurring in the way persons viewed retirement, so that as these views changed, so did the retirement locations that seemed attractive. These alternative possibilities should be explored when better data are available.

Although they are not presented here, the simple correlations between current and past migration variables for persons aged 65-69 and those aged 70+ follow very closely those of all elderly persons. The difference in migration patterns between young and older persons, then, results from a change in movements of all elderly persons, not simply those currently retiring or those who had retired in the past. This result makes the second suggestion proposed in the above paragraph less likely than the first. Differences between the correlation coefficients for males and females also are very minor.

*Migration Elasticities*

Migration elasticities of the migration variables appear in Table 4-3. They are calculated on the logarithms of the variables, and will not appear unless they are significant at the .05 level of confidence.

The elasticities for previous in- and out-migration are generally significant in explaining current in- and out-migration, respectively. (The exception is the unexpected appearance of past out-migration in the equation for in-migration of persons aged 65-69.) An increase of 1 percent in in-migration of persons aged 65 and over in 1949-1950 is associated with an increase of .82 percent in-migration of this group in 1955-1960. The elasticity for out-migration is less than that of in-migration.

*Influence of Elderly Widows*

Migration elasticities for males and females are about the same in each of the in-migration equations, but this is not true for out-migration. In both age

**Table 4-3**

**Migration-Rate Elasticities of Past Migration Variables in Gross Migration Equations for Elderly Persons**

| Migration Rates | $X_1$ | $X_2$ | $X_3$ |
|---|---|---|---|
| Gross In-Migration Males Aged 65+ | .79* | | |
| Gross In-Migration Females Aged 65+ | .88* | | |
| Gross In-Migration Total Aged 65+ | .82* | | |
| Gross Out-Migration Males Aged 65+ | | .37* | |
| Gross Out-Migration Females Aged 65+ | −.49 | .92* | |
| Gross Out-Migration Total Aged 65+ | | .32* | |
| Gross In-Migration Males Aged 65-69 | .88* | | |
| Gross In-Migration Females Aged 65-69 | .79* | | |
| Gross In-Migration Total Aged 65-69 | | .94 | |
| Gross Out-Migration Males Aged 65-69 | | .28* | |
| Gross Out-Migration Females Aged 65-69 | −1.41 | 1.81* | 29.84 |
| Gross Out-Migration Total Aged 65-69 | | .35* | |

*Expected sign.

groupings, the migration elasticity for females is much larger than for males, and for some reason, negative coefficients appear in these equations relating current out-migration to past in-migration. These two negative coefficients (−.49 and −1.41) suggest that not only is current out-migration a positive function of past out-migration, but it also is a negative function of past in-migration.

The higher migration elasticities for females and the appearance of the past in-migration variable could possibly be explained (and we offer this hypothesis cautiously) by the larger number of widows than widowers in the elderly population. Elderly widowed women may be more likely to move to another state to be near their children than elderly women whose husbands are living. Since states experiencing high out-migration in 1949-1950 will have larger numbers of mothers whose children live in other states (migration rates of younger persons exceed those of older persons), one would perhaps expect much greater response of women to prior out-migration rates. Undoubtedly, a substantial part of in-migration in most states is migration of persons returning to the home states of their parents. High in-migration rates would be expected, therefore to result in lower out-migration rates of widowed elderly women (ceteris paribus).

Past net migration elasticities $(X_3)$ appear in Table 4-3 only for females aged 65-69. The size of this elasticity—29.84—appears startling at first. But this is not a true elasticity. It is the elasticity of gross out-migration with respect to the past migration rate plus unity.

**Net Migration Rates.** Net migration of older persons between 1955 and 1960 is not as closely related to past net migration as are the gross population movements. Table 4-4 contains only those groups of persons for which the relationship between "current" net migration rates are significant.

While relatively few of the age and sex groupings appear in Table 4-4 it seems significant that in only three cases—net migration of all persons aged 70 and above—do variables other than past net migration enter, and the highest migration elasticity is only .01. Past gross migration rates do not appear to be closely associated with current net migration rates when other influences acting on migration are taken into account.

Past net migration enters only once for the six equations encompassing all elderly persons and those between ages 65 and 69. The appearance of past net migration in all three equations relating to persons aged 70 and over does not necessarily indicate these persons are affected differently by past migration than other age groups. Their presence could simply be due to the fact that the net migration rates for the oldest group cover the entire decade, 1950-1960, and could, therefore, be expected to be more closely associated with the 1949-1950 rates than net migration rates for 1955-1960.

Table 4-4
**Migration-Rate Coefficients of Past Migration Variables in Net Migration Equations of Elderly Persons**

| Net Migration Rates | $X_1$ | $X_2$ | $X_3$ |
|---|---|---|---|
| Males Aged 65+ | | | 2.54* |
| Females Aged 65+ | | | 2.54* |
| Persons Aged 65+ | | | 1.67* |
| Males Aged 70+ | .01 | | .27* |
| Females Aged 70+ | | .003 | .27* |
| Persons Aged 70+ | .004 | | .22* |

*Expected sign.

**Younger Persons.** Migration elasticities for persons under age 65 appear in Table 4-5, and generally follow the pattern of other age groups. Past in-migration appears in current in-migration equations, past out- with current out-migration, and past net with current net migration. One main difference in migration elasticities between the younger and older groups appears. Elasticities for males and females in the out-migration equations are of similar magnitudes for younger persons, whereas in both groups of older persons those for females are more than twice as large as those for males. The presence of the relatively large elasticity for females among older persons and its absence among younger persons lends some support to our supposition that migration patterns of elderly widows might account for the elasticity differences between the sexes of older age groups.

## Conclusions

We proposed three explanations for expecting to find a high association between past and current migration rates. While our data are not of the type that would allow us to distinguish the relative importance of these explanations, we have been able to test our expectations.

We find that gross in- and gross out-migration rates of persons between 1949 and 1950 are closely related to respective gross in- and gross out-migration rates

**Table 4-5**
**Migration-Rate Elasticities of Past Migration Persons Aged 64 and Under**

| Migration Rates | $X_1$ | $X_2$ | $X_3$ |
|---|---|---|---|
| Gross In-Migration | | | |
| Males | .78* | | |
| Females | .84* | | |
| Total | .83* | | |
| Gross Out-Migration | | | |
| Males | | .52* | |
| Females | | .45* | |
| Total | | .55* | |
| Net Migration | | | |
| Males | | | 2.92* |
| Females | | | 2.33* |
| Total | | | 1.50* |

*Expected sign.

of elderly persons in the period 1955 to 1960. While less consistent, net migration rates in the two periods are also related. What is not clear is how these relationships should be interpreted. At this point all our data suggest is that it is possible to predict gross migration rates among the states in some later period with a high degree of accuracy knowing nothing more than values for past migration rates. Many unanswered questions remain concerning this relationship.

## Note

1. Michael Greenwood, "Lagged Response in the Decision to Migrate," *Journal of Regional Science* 10, 3 (December 1970): 375-84.

# 5 Public Sector Influences on Migration

## Introduction

The elderly comprise a particularly appropriate group on which to test the influence of the public sector on locational decisions for two reasons. First, it is plausible that the public sector preferences of elderly persons are more homogeneous within the group than are the preferences of the population as a whole, so that by concentrating on this group one can more clearly discern the relationship between public sector variation and migration. For example, the elderly might be expected to be less concerned with expenditures on education and more concerned with expenditures on health care facilities than the general population; or, since many older persons have little current income (financing consumption out of wealth and transfer payments) they might be expected to be affected less by income taxes than by property taxes, relative to the general population.

The second reason that elderly persons might be strongly influenced by the public sector is that they have less attachment to the private sector of the economy, and so can give more weight to the public sector in making locational choices. Younger families, however, still relying principally on labor income, must compromise their public sector preferences with private sector opportunities. In contrast, social security benefits, annuity income, dividends, interest, and rental income can be received in any location. Families which are more reliant on these sources of income, or simply on depletion of wealth to finance consumption, are freer to choose their residential locations on the basis of public sector preferences.

Quite unexpectedly, we find that the public sector variables apparently exert only a minor influence on migration patterns of elderly persons. Not only do they rarely appear in our multiple regression equations, but they also have relatively low simple correlations with such migration. Either other considerations outweigh influences of the public sector or we have failed to measure adequately the relevant aspects of the public sector (either through omission of truly important variables or poor measurement of those we included).

## Description of Independent Variables

The nine public sector variables we use are identified below.

53

$X_{55}$ = Minimum number of years of residence required for old age assistance eligibility, 1950-1960 average;

$X_{56}$ = Maximum monthly old age assistance payment for one person, 1950-1960 average;

$X_{57}$ = Dollar amount of special old age state income tax exemption, 1963;

$X_{58}$ = Dollar amount of special old age state income tax credit, 1963;

$X_{59}$ = Per capita state and local property tax receipts, 1957-1962 average;

$X_{60}$ = Per capita state and local income tax receipts, 1950-1960 average;

$X_{61}$ = Per capita state and local expenditures on education, 1950-1960 average;

$X_{62}$ = Per capita state and local expenditures on health and hospitals, 1950-1960 average;

$X_{63}$ = Per capita state and local expenditures on public welfare, 1950-1960 average.

As indicated earlier, the public sector variables suggest how attractive certain aspects of states' public sectors are to older persons. It is to be expected that items which act to reduce the level of required expenditures, increase either gross or net income, and make more available services which are important to the elderly will increase in-migration and reduce out-migration of this group. Likewise, variables which tend to increase living costs, reduce gross or net income, or indicate a relative unavailability of certain services should reduce in-migration and increase out-migration. Our descriptions of the expected direction of the effect of the effort of the public sector variables on migration will be for *in*-migration. In each case, the expected sign is opposite for out-migration.

## Old Age Assistance

The first two variables—state residency requirements for old age assistance eligibility, and maximum old age assistance payment ($X_{55}$ and $X_{56}$)—describe the relative generosity of state old age assistance programs. We suggest that less strict residency requirements and higher maximum benefit levels should be associated with greater in-migration rates. If these expectations are realized, $X_{55}$ will have a negative migration elasticity and $X_{56}$ a positive migration elasticity.

## Tax Incentives

Variables $X_{57}$ and $X_{58}$ reflect special income and property tax advantages for elderly persons. Positive in-migration elasticities are expected for both of them.

While 17 states gave special income tax exemptions for persons aged 65 and over in 1963, only 4 gave tax credits (Table 5-1). Arizona gave the largest tax exemption ($1,000). The most common exemption (when it was given) was $600. The largest tax credit ($20) was granted by Kentucky; other states granting credits were Minnesota, Oregon, and Wisconsin. Given the small size of the tax credits it probably is too much to expect them to influence locational choices. While income tax exemptions are large relative to income levels of older persons, the generally low state income tax rates probably make actual tax savings from this source small. Unless the large visibility of the tax exemption itself influences migration, this variable also will probably have small impact on migration.

*Tax Levels*

Per capita state and local receipts from property taxes and from income taxes (variables $X_{59}$ and $X_{60}$ respectively) are expected to be inversely related to in-migration rates. Of course, income taxes tend to reduce spendable income of the elderly. Property taxes both increase living costs (in the form of higher rent or property tax payments) and reduce net income (in the form of lower net receipts from property income).

Property taxes are by far the larger income producers for states, with all states receiving revenue from this source. Per capita property tax receipts were highest in New York at $167 and lowest in Alabama at $24. Mean per capita property tax receipts in 1963 were $8,521. Only 33 states received revenues from income taxes between 1950 and 1960, and the mean per capita amount received by those with income taxes was $17.02.

Only Delaware received more income from income taxes than from property

**Table 5-1**
**Income Tax Exemptions and Credits, 1963**

| Exemptions | | Credits | |
|---|---|---|---|
| Amount | Number of States | Amount | Number of States |
| $1,000 | 1 | $20 | 1 |
| 800 | 2 | 15 | 1 |
| 750 | 1 | 12 | 1 |
| 600 | 11 | 10 | 1 |
| 500 | 2 | 0 | 44 |
| 0 | 31 | | |

Source: Yung-Ping Chen, "Income Tax Exemptions for the Aged as a Policy Instrument," *National Tax Journal* 16 (December 1963): 325-36.

**Table 5-2**
**Per Capita Property and Income Tax Receipts**

| | Property Tax[a] | | Income Tax[b] | |
| --- | --- | --- | --- | --- |
| | Amount | Number of States | Amount | Number of States |
| | $150 - $200 | 1 | $50 and over | 2 |
| | 100 - 149 | 17 | 25 - 49 | 5 |
| | 75 - 99 | 12 | 1 - 24 | 26 |
| | 50 - 74 | 5 | 0 | 15 |
| | 25 - 49 | 12 | | |
| | 0 - 24 | 1 | | |

[a]Average of 1957 and 1962.

[b]Average of 1950 and 1960.

Source: U.S. Department of Commerce, Bureau of the Budget, *Compendium of State Government Finances*, various (Washington, D.C.: U.S. Government Printing Office), Table 5.

taxes, and its $55 per capita income tax receipts were the highest of all states. Most states received less than $24 (per capita) from income taxes. The influence of property taxes on migration is expected to be more discernable than that of income taxes. Property taxes are the more important source of state revenues and cannot be "avoided" by failure to have earned income.

*Expenditures on Education, Medical Care, and Public Welfare*

The last three public sector variables—per capita state and local expenditures on education ($X_{61}$), health and hospitals ($X_{62}$) and public welfare ($X_{63}$)—partially describe the mix of public goods provided, and represent potential "offsets" to income and property tax payments. Elderly persons are unlikely to have school-age children. Consequently, state and local government expenditures for education (variable $X_{61}$) act simply to increase taxes without yielding proportionate offsetting benefits.[a] A negative migration elasticity is expected for this variable. On the other hand, persons over age 65 are relatively important beneficiaries of health and hospital services, and of public welfare expenditures.

[a]We are not arguing that elderly persons receive no benefits from public expenditures on education. They are in fact the direct recipients of certain education expenditures when they utilize public school and university facilities for community activities and for adult education programs. They benefit from cultural and sports activities provided by schools. Finally, they share in increased output of goods and services as education provides educated and skilled persons to labor markets.

Our variables $X_{62}$ and $X_{63}$ serve as proxies for the availability of these services.[b] Positive migration elasticities should accompany both these variables. Per capita expenditures for education, health and hospitals, and for public welfare appear in Table 5-3.

**Statistical Results**

As a group, the public sector variables exert little influence on the locational choice of older persons. Few of the variables have statistically significant relationships with migration; many of those relationships which are significant are not the expected type.

*Simple Correlation Coefficients*

Table 5-4 contains the simple correlation coefficients between migration rates of elderly persons and each of the nine public sector variables. Significant coefficients are underlined and coefficients with signs confirming our expectations are indicated by asterisks. These coefficients for dollar amounts of special old age state income tax credit $(X_{58})$, per capita state and local income tax receipts $(X_{60})$, per capita state and local expenditures on health and hospitals $(X_{62})$ and per capita state and local expenditures on public welfare $(X_{63})$ are

**Table 5-3**
**Per Capita State and Local Expenditures on Education, Health and Hospitals, and Public Welfare, 1950-1960 Average**

| Education | | Health and Hospitals | | Public Welfare | |
|---|---|---|---|---|---|
| Amount | Number of States | Amount | Number of States | Amount | Number of States |
| Greater than $99 | 12 | Greater than $19 | 9 | Greater than $49 | 2 |
| 75 to 99 | 20 | 15 - 19 | 16 | 25 - 49 | 12 |
| 50 - 74 | 16 | 10 - 14 | 21 | Less than 25 | 34 |
| Less than 50 | 0 | Less than 10 | 2 | | |

Source: U.S. Department of Commerce, Bureau of the Budget, *Compendium of State Government Finances*, various (Washington, D.C.: U.S. Government Printing Office).

[b]Our variable for health and hospital services fails to isolate the influence of price differences from differences in quantities of health services supplied. Better data are available should this research be continued.

**Table 5-4**
**Simple Correlation Coefficients[a] between the Public Sector Variables and Migration Rates**

| Migration Rates | | | | Public Sector Variables | | | | | |
|---|---|---|---|---|---|---|---|---|---|
| | $X_{55}$ | $X_{56}$ | $X_{57}$ | $X_{58}$ | $X_{59}$ | $X_{60}$ | $X_{61}$ | $X_{62}$ | $X_{63}$ |
| Gross In-Migration, Males Aged 65+ | .311 | .106* | .157* | -.115 | .001 | -.011* | .300 | -.046 | -.146 |
| Gross In-Migration, Females Aged 65+ | .315 | .189* | .223* | -.115 | .135 | -.018* | .364 | .059* | -.185 |
| Gross In-Migration, Total Aged 65+ | .315 | .150* | .193* | -.118 | .072 | -.016* | .331 | .011* | -.170 |
| Gross Out-Migration, Males Aged 65+ | .073* | .276 | .241 | -.113* | .479* | -.152 | .237* | .215 | -.115* |
| Gross Out-Migration, Females Aged 65+ | .086* | .354 | .308 | -.087* | .438* | -.072 | .231* | .121 | -.155* |
| Gross Out-Migration, Total Aged 65+ | .040* | .257 | .258 | -.123* | .448* | -.152 | .202* | .102 | -.161* |
| Gross In-Migration, Males Aged 65-69 | .325 | .067* | .126* | -.091 | -.019 | .007 | .330 | -.050 | -.141 |
| Gross In-Migration, Females Aged 65-69 | .338 | .135* | .175* | -.099 | .096 | -.011* | .341 | .045* | -.175 |
| Gross In-Migration, Total Aged 65-69 | .332 | .102* | .151* | -.097 | .040 | -.004* | .335 | -.001 | -.161 |
| Gross Out-Migration, Males Aged 65-69 | .087* | .319 | .253 | -.102* | .500* | -.149 | .286* | .218 | -.057* |
| Gross Out-Migration, Females Aged 65-69 | .074* | .266 | .231 | -.081* | .437* | -.128 | .213* | .161 | -.127* |
| Gross Out-Migration, Total Aged 65-69 | .080* | .295 | .245 | -.093* | .473* | -.141 | .250* | .191 | -.096* |

*Expected sign.

[a]Single underlining indicates significance at .05 confidence level; double underlining indicates significance at .01 level.

not significant at the .05 confidence level for any of the migration rates. The coefficient for $X_{57}$ (amount of special old age state income tax exemption) is significant for only 1 of the 12 migration rates in this table, and it has the wrong sign.

The remaining four variables ($X_{55}$, $X_{56}$, $X_{59}$, and $X_{61}$) display fairly consistent patterns. They are generally significant for in- or for out-migration rates, but not for both. All 48 coefficients for these 4 variables (4 variables times 12 equations) are positive, so that half have the expected sign and half do not. In most cases, the signs of significant coefficients are contrary to those predicted. Only per capita state and local property tax receipts ($X_{59}$) has coefficients that consistently are significant *and* have the expected sign. This last result suggests that if other influences on migration are ignored, high per capita property taxes induce out-migration of the elderly. The positive simple relationship between property taxes and out-migration is equally strong for elderly persons aged 65-69, for all persons over 65, and for both sexes taken individually for each age group.

## Migration Elasticity

Table 5-5 contains the estimated migration elasticities for the public sector variables. As before, these elasticities come from complete regression equations containing all of our variables. Elasticities with the expected signs are indicated by asterisks.

**Property Tax Receipts.** Most of the cells in Table 5-5 are empty, indicating that the public sector variables rarely satisfied the .05 significance criterion required to enter the equations. A comparison between the significant simple coefficients in Table 5-4 with the migration elasticities which appear in Table 5-5 reveals that out of the 24 significant coefficients in the earlier table, only 2 also appear in Table 5-5. Neither of these coefficients has the expected sign. The only independent variable giving consistent, predicted results in Table 5-4 ($X_{59}$, property tax receipts), is not significant in any of the 12 equations in Table 5-5.

The apparent influence of high per capita property taxes on out-migration of older persons disappears partly because property taxes are highly correlated with a binary variable for geography (states below the 37th parallel have the value 2 while states above the parallel have the value 1 for this variable) discussed later in this report. Each time the geography variable enters a regression equation, the partial correlation between property taxes and migration rates becomes insignificant.

**Expenditures on Health and Hospitals.** Most entries in Table 5-5 are for variables which have no significant simple correlations with the migration rates

**Table 5-5**
**Migration-Rate Elasticities[a] of Public Sector Variables in Gross Migration Equations for the Elderly**

| Migration Rates | Public Sector Variables[b] | | | | | |
|---|---|---|---|---|---|---|
| | $X_{56}$ | $X_{57}$ | $X_{58}$ | $X_{60}$ | $X_{62}$ | $X_{63}$ |
| Gross In-Migration, Males Aged 65+ | | | | .05 | | -.38 |
| Gross In-Migration, Females Aged 65+ | | | | .05 | -.39 | -.30 |
| Gross In-Migration, Total Aged 65+ | | | | | -.26 | -.21 |
| Gross Out-Migration, Males Aged 65+ | | .02 | | -.05 | | |
| Gross Out-Migration, Females Aged 65+ | .22 | .02 | | | | -.21* |
| Gross In-Migration, Males Aged 65-69 | | | | .07 | -.97 | |
| Gross In-Migration, Females Aged 65-69 | | | | .06 | -1.00 | |
| Gross In-Migration, Total Aged 65-69 | | | | .10 | -.64 | -.28 |
| Gross Out-Migration, Males Aged 65-69 | | | -.11* | | | |
| Gross Out-Migration, Females Aged 65-69 | | .02 | | -.05 | | |
| Gross Out-Migration, Total Aged 65-69 | | | | -.05 | | |

*Expected sign.

[a]All elasticities are significant at .05 confidence level.

[b]Defined in text. Variables $X_{55}$, $X_{59}$, and $X_{61}$ do not enter these equations.

$(X_{60}, X_{62},$ and $X_{63})$, and only two coefficients are significant in both tables. Additionally, (absolute) elasticities for variables $X_{56}, X_{57}, X_{60},$ and $X_{63}$ are low; the highest for any of these variables is .38. On the other hand, migration elasticities for $X_{62}$ (per capita expenditures on health and hospitals) are relatively large. The sign of each elasticity for health and hospital expenditures is, however, opposite to that hypothesized. Rather than encouraging in-migration, high per capita expenditures for health care appear to strongly discourage in-migration.

Given the possibility that per capita expenditures on health and hospitals may not be a dependable proxy for the availability of health care, we cannot conclude that increased availability of health care discourages in-migration of elderly persons. Per capita expenditures may be high because of generally high costs of living (a variable we were unsuccessful in building into our migration equations), and it may be the latter influence which is acting to decrease in-migration. Or, high expenditures for health care may represent a population with a high incidence of illness, a situation which might discourage in-migration. A final possibility suggests itself. We may have interpreted the implications of high per capita expenditures on health and hospitals incorrectly. Rather than representing states with a relative abundance of health services, they may represent states which are straining the health industry's capacity to supply services. If this alternative interpretation is true, then the results do suggest that elderly persons attempt to live in areas with relatively available health care.

*Public Sector Variables in Isolation*

Since our results above are so unexpected, we ran two additional variations on our equations. First, we calculated a multiple regression equation in which *only* the public sector variables were included, forcing in all 9 variables regardless of whether they were statistically significant. Second, we used the 9 public sector variables in a step-wise regression equation which again excluded all other variables, but excluded any variable not significant at the .05 confidence level. The results are consistent with our findings discussed above.

Table 5-6 contains the significant coefficients between public sector variables and migration rates when only public sector variables are allowed to enter the regression equations. Results contained in Table 5-6 reaffirm our conclusion that public sector variables exert little influence on migration patterns of the elderly. Few variables appear at all, and half have unpredicted signs. Two coefficients of determination appear. The higher one results when all public sector variables are included regardless of whether they are significant; the lower one results when only the significant variables are used. Even when all 9 variables are included, the $R^2$s are relatively low. Public sector variables can "explain" only 30 percent of the variation in in-migration rates of persons aged 65 and over (29 percent for

**Table 5-6**
**Migration-Rate Elasticities of Public-Sector Variables for Persons Aged 65 and Over When Other Variables are Excluded[a]**

| | Public Sector Variables | | | | |
| Migration Rates | $X_{57}$ | $X_{59}$ | $X_{61}$ | $R^2$ [b] | $R^2$ [c] |
|---|---|---|---|---|---|
| Gross In-Migration Persons Aged 65+ | | | − .43 | .30 | .17 |
| Gross Out-Migration Persons Aged 65+ | .03 | .34* | | .40 | .27 |
| Gross In-Migration Persons Aged 65-69 | | | 1.04 | .29 | .11 |
| Gross Out-Migration Persons Aged 65-69 | | .37* | | .40 | .22 |

*Predicted sign.

[a]Variables $X_{55}$, $X_{56}$, $X_{58}$, $X_{60}$, and $X_{63}$ are not significant at the .05 level of confidence.

[b]Coefficients of determination resulting when all variables $X_{55}$-$X_{63}$ are included in equations, regardless of their significance.

[c]Coefficients of determination resulting when only significant (at the .05 level of confidence) variables shown in table are included.

persons between age 65 and 69), and 40 percent of the variation in out-migration. When only significant variables are included, the $R^2$s fall substantially. Those for in- and out-migration equations relating to all older persons fall from .30 and .40, to .17 and .27, respectively. Those for the subgroup of persons aged 65-69 fall from .29 and .40, to .11 and .22, respectively.

As might be expected, per capita property tax receipts ($X_{59}$) have significant elasticity coefficients of the predicted sign—high tax levels are associated with high out-migration. Recall, however, that property taxes disappear as a significant variable in a more complete equation. Only one other variable, $X_{61}$, has a migration elasticity of the expected sign. High expenditures on education seem to discourage in-migration of older persons as a group. The very high elasticity for education expenditures when related to persons aged 65-69 cannot be explained. Apparently educational expenditures are standing in for some variable, not included in this set of equations, that has a strong influence on in-migration of persons in this age group but little influence on persons over age 70.

*Younger Persons*

There is good reason to expect persons under age 65 to react differently to public sector variables than those aged 65 and over. One would expect younger persons' reactions to be weaker; smaller proportions of their incomes are related to public sector variables, and private sector involvement is much stronger. One also would expect younger persons to react to different variables. For example, state old age provisions should be of little consideration for younger persons.

**Simple Correlation Coefficients.** As suggested above, any significant relationships would not be expected to emerge between migration patterns of younger persons and public sector variables which relate specifically to the elderly. This expectation is substantially satisfied in Table 5-7. Simple correlation coefficients between $X_{55}$, $X_{56}$, $X_{57}$, and $X_{58}$ are insignificant with the exception of in-migration and years' residency requirement for old age assistance. None of these four coefficients is significant at the .01 level. Reactions of persons under age 65 to state per capita property and income tax receipts ($X_{59}$ and $X_{60}$) should be similar to those of older persons. Unexpectedly, this is not the case. Elderly persons are migrating out of states with high property taxes. Younger persons are migrating into these states (although the latter relationship is not statistically significant). Neither broad age group, however, reacts strongly to per capita income tax rates.

Unlike elderly persons, who should be repulsed by high expenditures on education, younger families are expected to benefit greatly from such expenditures and should migrate into states with high expenditures on education. Simple correlation coefficients between $X_{61}$ and in-migration are indeed positive and significant at the .01 confidence level.

Relative abundance of health and hospital services should attract younger persons. While the simple coefficients are not significant for in-migration, they are significant and of the expected sign for out-migration. Fewer younger persons move away from states with relatively high expenditures in health and hospitals. We held no firm expectations for the association between welfare payments and migration of younger persons. While all of the coefficients are negative, none is significant.

**Migration Elasticities.** Results of our complete migration equations for younger persons appear in Table 5-8. Results fail to bear out our expectations. While 6 of the 9 public sector variables enter the equations, only 2 of the coefficients have the predicted signs.

**Public Sector Variables in Isolation.** Equations developed solely from public sector variables behave as predicted (Table 5-4), and the migration elasticities appear in Table 5-9. Younger persons are encouraged to migrate into a state with relatively high education expenditures (elasticity of .58) and discouraged from moving from a state with high health care expenditures (elasticity of −.35). Both elasticities are of the expected signs.

Total proportions of explained migration are low. When all public sector

**Table 5-7**
**Simple Correlation Coefficients Between Public Sector Variables and Migration Rates of Younger Persons**

| Migration Rates | | Public Sector Variables | | | | | | | |
| --- | --- | --- | --- | --- | --- | --- | --- | --- | --- |
| | $X_{55}$ | $X_{56}$ | $X_{57}$ | $X_{58}$ | $X_{59}$ | $X_{60}$ | $X_{61}$ | $X_{62}$ | $X_{63}$ |
| Gross In-Migration Males Aged 64- | .278 | .176 | .195 | -.161 | .032 | -.000* | .373* | -.015 | -.048 |
| Gross In-Migration Females Aged 64- | .319 | .228 | .215 | -.154 | .116 | .016 | .427* | .015 | -.028 |
| Gross In-Migration Persons Aged 64- | .299 | .201 | .205 | -.158 | .072 | .007 | .400* | -.001 | -.039 |
| Gross Out-Migration Males Aged 64- | .068 | .107 | .208 | -.133 | -.087 | -.030 | .173 | -.287* | -.008 |
| Gross Out-Migration Females Aged 64- | .034 | .123 | .238 | -.125 | -.082 | .002* | .148 | -.311* | -.022 |
| Gross Out-Migration Persons Aged 64- | .052 | .115 | .224 | -.130 | -.085 | -.014 | .161 | -.300* | -.015 |

*Expected sign.

**Table 5-8**
**Migration-Rate Elasticities of Public-Sector Variables in Equations for Persons Aged 64 and Under**

| Migration Rates | $X_{55}$ | $X_{56}$ | $X_{58}$ | $X_{59}$ | $X_{60}$ | $X_{62}$ |
|---|---|---|---|---|---|---|
| Gross In-Migration Males Aged 64- | | | | -.23* | | |
| Gross In-Migration Females Aged 64- | .08 | | | | | |
| Gross In-Migration Total Aged 64- | | | | | | -.21 |
| Gross Out-Migration Males Aged 64- | | .12 | | | -.02 | |
| Gross Out-Migration Females Aged 64- | | .15 | -.05* | | | |
| Gross Out-Migration Total Aged 64- | | .19 | | | | |

*Expected sign.

**Table 5-9**
**Migration-Rate Elasticities of Public-Sector Variables for Persons Aged 64 and Under when Other Variables are Excluded[a]**

| Migration Rates | $X_{61}$ | $X_{62}$ | $R^2$ [b] | $R^2$ [c] |
|---|---|---|---|---|
| Gross In-Migration Total Aged 64- | .58* | | .28 | .16 |
| Gross Out-Migration Total Aged 64- | | -.35* | .19 | .10 |

*Expected sign.

[a]Only variables $X_{61}$ and $X_{62}$ are significant at the .05 level of confidence.

[b]Coefficients of determination resulting when all variables ($X_{55}$-$X_{63}$) are included in equations, regardless of their significance.

[c]Coefficients of determination resulting when only significant (at the .05 level of confidence) are included.

variables are considered without regard to their significance, the $R^2$s for in- and out-migration rates are .28 and .19 respectively. When only significant variables are included, the $R^2$s fall to .16 and .10 respectively for the two directions of migration. In each case, public sector variables explain a smaller proportion of total migration of younger persons than of older. These differences are summarized in Table 5-10. The difference in the in-migration equation is small (.16 vs. .17), but that for out-migration is relatively large (.10 vs. .27). These

**Table 5-10**
**Coefficients of Determination for Equations Using Significant Public Sector Variables**

|  | $R^2$ |
| --- | --- |
| Gross In-Migration | |
| Total Aged 65+ | .17 |
| Total Aged 64- | .16 |
| Gross Out-Migration | |
| Total Aged 65+ | .27 |
| Total Aged 64- | .10 |

Source: Tables 5-6 and 5-9.

results are consistent with our expectations that the public sector variables we selected are more significant for older, than for younger, persons. Indeed, we would have been greatly surprised to find out differently. Most of these variables are selected with the elderly in mind and should be more relevant for their decisions on migration. Furthermore as argued above, younger persons should react less strongly to public sector variation than older persons.

## Conclusions

Our results regarding the impact of public sector variables on migration of the elderly suggest that elderly persons are influenced only slightly by availability and levels of state old age benefits and public welfare assistance, special tax treatment, overall tax levels, and availability of public health and hospital care. These results do not confirm a previously untested hypothesis proposed by Charles Tiebout in 1956 that the public sector will have substantial influence on migration patterns,[1] nor are they consistent with commonly expressed opinions about the relative importance of the public sector in the locational choice of the elderly.

Most simple correlations between the public sector variables and migration rates are either non-significant or have signs contrary to our expectations. Few public sector variables are significant in either our complete migration equations or those including only public sector variables.

In the complete equations, old age assistance residency requirements, maximum level of old age assistance payments, and expenditures on education did not appear at all. Special old age income tax exemptions, old age tax credits, and per capita property tax receipts appeared in only 1 of 12 equations each. Migration equations built using only public sector variables could explain only a small portion of total old-age migration patterns.

With a good portion of migration associated with retirement occurring between ages 65 and 69, we expected possible substantial differences in the way public sector variables affected this subgroup of elderly persons compared with all older persons. No significant differences can be found. Elderly persons making the migration decision upon retirement apparently pay as little attention to public sector variables as do older persons moving for other reasons.

When only public sector variables are considered, elderly persons are discouraged from migrating to states with high per capita expenditures on education, while younger persons are encouraged to migrate to these states.

As expected, younger persons' migration decisions apparently are not influenced by most of the public sector variables. But, unlike elderly persons, they behave as predicted with respect to variations in per capita property tax receipts among states.

## Note

1. Charles M. Tiebout, "A Pure Theory of Local Expenditures," *Journal of Political Economy* (October 1956), pp. 416-24.

# 6

# Influence of Income on Migration

Tabulations presented in Chapter 2 comparing elderly persons' incomes with their mobility status suggest that elderly persons with moderate income levels ($1,000 to $4,000 annually) are more likely to be "movers" than those with either lower *or higher* incomes (see Table 2-1). This apparent lower mobility of older persons with high incomes in surprising, and suggests that elderly persons' migration response to income may differ substantially from that of younger persons.

In this chapter we explore the nature of the relationships between migration of elderly persons and income, and compare the migration response of elderly persons to income with that of younger persons.

Simple correlation coefficients relating wage levels to migration suggest that the elderly are not strongly attracted to states by high wage income; that low incomes retard, and high incomes facilitate out-migration of older persons; and that younger persons react differently to wage and income signals than do older persons. Results from the multiple regression equations are less clear, and in many cases are counter to the hypotheses developed in this chapter. Differences in migration behavior between older and younger persons, however, remain clear.

## Income and Migration

There are two principal ways in which migration rates of elderly persons and income might be related:

1. to the extent they are attached to the labor force, elderly persons might migrate in search of superior employment opportunities, so that states with high wage rates would experience high rates of in-migration and low rates of out-migration of elderly persons, ceteris paribus, and
2. elderly persons with high incomes can more easily afford to migrate upon retirement.

These possibilities are discussed in more detail below.

*Wage Income*

Work by economists on movements of population has stressed the response of flows of migrants to differences in wage rates. The reason is that interregional population movements are thought to be one of the mechanisms by which the private enterprise economy achieves efficient allocation of resources. Regions which are relatively labor short (high marginal productivity of labor) should acquire more labor at the expense of regions with abundance of labor (low marginal productivity of labor). In this way total output is increased, since the movement reduces output in the labor-abundant regions by less than it increases output in the labor-short regions. The desired movement can be achieved without centralized direction, provided sufficiently many persons are willing and able to change their residences in order to earn higher wages. The hypothesis that regional movements are responsive to income differentials in the expected way has been verified, for example, by Larry A. Sjaastad.[1]

It is not necessary, of course, for the entire population to be mobile for the economic model of migration to operate. Only "marginal" workers need move in order to equalize marginal productivity among regions. In particular, it seems unlikely that many elderly persons move in search of higher wages.

In Chapter 1, data were presented which suggested that migration of elderly persons appears to be strongly associated with the retirement decision and withdrawal from the labor force. To the extent that withdrawal is voluntary, elderly persons will be relatively unconcerned with wage rates in alternative locations. To the extent that withdrawal is involuntary (we argued in Chapter 1 that there is not negligible amounts of involuntary withdrawal), persons probably will be more concerned with the availability of employment in alternative locations than with wage rates. We therefore do not expect migration rates of elderly persons to be strongly associated with wage rates, but we stress that this expectation is not at variance with the importance or validity of the economist's general approach to population mobility.

*Wealth*

The second possible reason for association between migration and income is that persons with considerable wealth can afford to move, while persons with little wealth cannot. Since wealth is accumulated from saving out of income it is reasonable to suppose that states with higher proportions of high-income persons will have larger proportions of persons with considerable wealth, than will states with larger proportions of low-income persons.

Costs of moving are certainly not negligible for a typical interstate relocation. It is easy to imagine that elderly persons with moderate wealth would be unwilling to spend a substantial portion of it on interstate migration. If this is so, out-migration rates of elderly persons should be lower for states where the elderly population has relatively low income, and higher for states where the elderly population has relatively high income. Except for mere statistical reasons, which are discussed below, we would not expect as strong relationships of any type between income and in-migration rates.

### Income Data

The income level of a state is determined by the combination of the following factors—level of wages paid in the various industries operating in the state, mix of employment among the various industries, level of unemployment, and amounts of non-labor income received by the residents of the state. We have chosen our income variables so that the effects of wage income on migration rates can be discerned separately from the effects of industry mix, levels of unemployment, and non-labor income.[a]

*Wage Income*

From the range of possible wage level variables available, we selected three. They are identified in Table 6-1. These variables were computed by dividing the total annual wages paid in each industry for the years available by the average level of

**Table 6-1**
**1950-1960 Average Wage Incomes in Manufacturing, FIRE, and Service**

| Wage Variables | Mean | Standard Deviation |
|---|---|---|
| Average Wages in Manufacturing, 1950-1960 average | $3,991 | $642 |
| Average Wages in Finance, Insurance, and Real Estate (FIRE), 1950-1960 average | $3,769 | $379 |
| Average Wages in Services, 1950-1960 average | $3,029 | $514 |

Source: Calculated from U.S. Department of Labor, Bureau of Labor Statistics, *Employment and Earnings Statistics for States and Areas (1939-1966)*, Bulletin No. 1370-4 (Washington, D.C.: U.S. Government Printing Office, 1967); U.S. Department of Commerce, Office of Business Economics, *Personal Income by State since 1929* (Washington, D.C.: U.S. Government Printing Office), Tables 6-62; U.S. Department of Commerce, Office of Business Economics, *Survey of Current Business* (Washington, D.C.: U.S. Government Printing Office, August, 1959), Tables 6-62, and ibid., August, 1961, Tables 6-62a.

[a]In fact, unemployment levels are considered in Chapter 7 where labor-maker factors which might influence migration are discussed.

employment in that industry. Annual data for each of the years between 1950 and 1960 are not available, so the average we use is the average of 1950, 1955, and 1960. Unless the two halves of the decade were characterized by wage movements of substantially different magnitudes, the averages as we have calculated them will yield reasonably accurate estimates of average annual wages between 1950 and 1960.

A serious difficulty in use of these annual wage income estimates in our migration model requires mention. These estimates refer to the labor force as a whole and may not represent the earnings potentials of elderly persons. It must be assumed that average wage incomes paid to elderly persons in these industries bear some regular relationship to computed average wages among the states for each of the three industry classifications.

*Median Income*

To represent the income levels of states with simple measures of central tendency we employ three variables. Two are specific to elderly persons, the third relates to all families. Census data are utilized to calculate these variables, and their means and standard deviations in Table 6-2 are based on a simple average of median incomes in 1949 and in 1959. Available data do not allow a calculation of incomes of families with elderly family heads by state, so we are unable to differentiate incomes of elderly persons living alone from joint incomes of those living together. We also are unable to identify separately the various sources of incomes; i.e., wages, property, and pensions and welfare. These are important shortcomings, because sources and levels of income

**Table 6-2**
**1949-1959 Average Median Income of Males and Females Aged 65 through 74 in 1960, and of All Families in 1960**

| Income Variable | Mean | Standard Deviation |
|---|---|---|
| 1949-1959 Average Median Income of Males Aged 65-74 in 1960 | $2,142 | $473 |
| 1949-1959 Average Median Income of Females Aged 65-74 in 1960 | $ 861 | $179 |
| 1949-1959 Average Median Income of All Families | $4,069 | $781 |

Source: Calculated from U.S. Department of Commerce, Bureau of the Census, *U.S. Census of Population, 1960*, Vol. 1, *Characteristics of the Population*, Parts 2-52 (Washington, D.C.: U.S. Government Printing Office, 1960), Table 141, and ibid., *Census of Population, 1950*, Vol. II, *Characteristics of the Population*, Parts 2-50, Tables 32 and 89.

probably vary substantially among the three main groups of elderly persons (single men, single women, and couples), and differences in the sources of income may have substantial effects on migration behavior.

*Income Distribution*

We use a simple four-category income distribution to provide additional detail concerning the incomes of elderly persons.

$X_{13}$ = Proportion of persons aged 65 and older whose 1959 incomes were less than $3,000;

$X_{14}$ = Proportion of persons aged 65 and older whose 1959 incomes were greater than $2,999 and less than $6,000;

$X_{15}$ = Proportion of persons aged 65 and older whose 1959 incomes were greater than $5,999 and less than $10,000;

$X_{16}$ = Proportion of persons aged 65 and older whose 1959 incomes were greater than $9,999.

Means and standard deviations of these four variables appear in Table 6-3. Over half of all elderly persons received incomes under $3,000 in 1959; 8 percent received incomes in excess of $10,000. The coefficient of variation for variable $X_{16}$ (the proportion of elderly persons with incomes over $10,000 in 1959) substantially exceeds those for variables $X_{13}$, $X_{14}$, and $X_{15}$. This indicates that elderly persons with extremely high incomes are less evenly distributed among the states than are elderly persons with lower incomes. Somewhat surprisingly, elderly persons of moderate incomes (variable $X_{14}$) are more diffused through-

Table 6-3
**Proportions of Persons Aged 65 and Over with Income Levels in Selected Categories, 1959**

| Income Level | Mean | Standard Deviation | Coefficient of Variation |
|---|---|---|---|
| Less than $3,000 | .510 | .106 | 20.8 |
| $3,000 - $5,999 | .275 | .043 | 16.0 |
| $6,000 - $9,999 | .135 | .040 | 29.6 |
| $10,000 and over | .080 | .033 | 41.2 |

Source: U.S. Department of Commerce, Bureau of the Census, *U.S. Census of Population, 1960: Subject Reports, Income of Elderly Population*, Final Report PC(2)-8B (Washington, D.C.: U.S. Government Printing Office), Table 6.

out the states than those with the lowest incomes (variable $X_{13}$). A possible explanation for differences in the coefficients of variation of variables $X_{13}$ - $X_{16}$ is proposed later in the chapter.


## Empirical Results

Our expectations with respect to the wage income variables ($X_7$ - $X_9$) were that no significant relationship between wage levels and migration rates of elderly persons would be discovered, for reasons described earlier. We did, however, expect that in-migration rates of non-elderly persons might be positively correlated with wage incomes, while out-migration rates might be negatively correlated.

We expected to find no correlation between the median income variables ($X_{10}$ - $X_{12}$) and in-migration, and a positive correlation between these variables and out-migration.

We predicted that variable $X_{13}$ (proportion of elderly persons with annual incomes below $3,000) would be negatively correlated to out-migration rates, and that variable $X_{16}$ (proportion of elderly persons with annual incomes of $10,000 or more) would be positively correlated with out-migration. We had no firm expectations concerning the effects of variable $X_{14}$ and $X_{15}$ on migration rates of the elderly.


### Simple Correlation Coefficients

Simple correlation coefficients relating the ten income variables to migration rates of elderly and non-elderly persons are contained in Table 6-4. Our expectations concerning the effects of income and wages on migration rates are largely borne out by these coefficients. First consider the wage income variables.

**Wage Incomes.** The coefficients of manufacturing and of finance, insurance, and real estate (FIRE) wage incomes ($X_7$ and $X_8$) with respect to in-migration of persons aged 65 and over and aged 65-69 are not significantly different from zero. The coefficients of service wages with respect to the same migration rates, however, *are* significant (and positive) and this result is counter to our expectations. Ignoring other factors which may attract the elderly, high incomes of persons employed in service industries seem to induce in-migration of this group.

We should further note that the coefficients of all the wage variables with respect to out-migration rates of persons aged 65 and older and aged 65-69 are positive. This is not what one would expect from the usual model of migration. This result can be understood, however, if high wage rates result in high incomes

**Table 6-4**
**Simple Correlation Coefficients between Average Wage Incomes, 1950-1960, and Migration**

| Migration Rate | Industry | | |
|---|---|---|---|
| | Manufacturing $(X_7)$ | FIRE $(X_8)$ | Services $(X_9)$ |
| Gross In-Migration Persons Aged 65+ | .062 | .225 | .332a |
| Gross Out-Migration Persons Aged 65+ | .324 | .164 | .029 |
| Gross In-Migration Persons Aged 65-69 | .047 | .211 | .353 |
| Gross Out-Migration Persons Aged 65-69 | .411 | .205 | .090 |
| Gross In-Migration Persons Aged 64- | .106 | .176 | .302* |
| Gross Out-Migration Persons Aged 64- | −.138 | −.341* | −.290* |

*Predicted sign.

aCoefficients underlined once are significant at the .05 level of significance, and those underlined twice are significant at the .01 level of significance.

during and after one's working years, and if persons with high incomes after retirement are more likely to move than persons with low incomes.

**Total Incomes.** Expectations concerning the action of the total income variables $(X_{10} - X_{16})$ are largely fulfilled. None of the median income variables $(X_{10} - X_{12})$ or the income distribution variables $(X_{15} - X_{16})$ is significantly related to in-migration of either elderly group. On the other hand, the simple coefficients between median incomes of elderly persons and out-migration are positive and significant at the .01 level of confidence (Table 6-5).

As expected, nearly every coefficient of correlation relating income distribution variables to out-migration rates of elderly persons is significant. The only nonsignificant variable is that relating out-migration of elderly persons with the proportion of such persons having annual incomes of $10,000 or more. This coefficient—.273—is only .02 from being significant at the .05 level of confidence.

We are surprised to find higher correlations between out-migration of elderly persons and variables $X_{14}$ and $X_{15}$ than between out-migration and variable $X_{16}$; the reverse was expected. These results suggest that only moderate income is required for an elderly person or couple to be able to afford interstate migration. Negative coefficients for $X_{13}$ (proportion of elderly persons with

**Table 6-5**
**Simple Correlation Coefficients between Annual Income (1949-1959) and Migration Rates**

| | Median Incomes | | | Proportions of Elderly Persons in Specific Income Categories | | | |
|---|---|---|---|---|---|---|---|
| | Males Aged 65+ $(X_{10})$ | Females Aged 65+ $(X_{11})$ | All Families $(X_{12})$ | Under $3,000 $(X_{13})$ | $3,000-$5,999 $(X_{14})$ | $6,000-$9,999 $(X_{15})$ | $10,000 and over $(X_{16})$ |
| Gross In-Migration | | | | | | | |
| Persons Aged 65+ | .133 | .202 | .144 | -.191 | .256 | .146 | .176 |
| Persons Aged 65-69 | .093 | .175 | .116 | -.151 | .198 | .102 | .162 |
| Persons Aged 64- | .147 | .206 | .170 | -.174 | .241 | .137 | .175 |
| Gross Out-Migration | | | | | | | |
| Persons Aged 65+ | .507*a | .408* | .423* | -.445* | .535 | .416* | .273* |
| Persons Aged 65-69 | .574* | .470* | .510* | -.515* | .571 | .495* | .360* |
| Persons Aged 64- | -.088 | -.189 | -.175 | .212 | .012 | -.224 | -.323 |

*Predicted sign.

aCoefficients underlined once are significant at the .05 level of confidence; those underlined twice are significant at the .01 level of confidence.

incomes below $3,000) indicate that elderly persons with very low incomes tend not to change their states of residence.

**Older Versus Younger Persons.** It is interesting to contrast the coefficients of correlation relating migration of elderly persons to wage rates with those relating migration of non-elderly persons to wage rates (variables $X_7$ - $X_9$). For the younger group, in- and out-migration rates are related oppositely to wage rates. In-migration rates are higher in high-wage states, lower in low-wage states. In contrast, out-migration rates are lower in high-wage states, higher in low-wage states. This result is expected from the usual economic model of migration. The appearance of negative coefficients for out-migration of younger persons in the wage income variables, compared to the positive coefficients for older persons in out-migration equations confirms our hypothesis that elderly persons are less concerned than non-elderly persons with earnings potentials of different wage levels.

The median income variables in Table 6-4 have no significant relation to in-migration for either of the elderly groups or for the non-elderly group. While the simple correlation coefficients are significant and positive for out-migration rates of both groups of elderly persons, they are negative (but not significant) for the non-elderly group.[b] Again, out-migration of persons aged 64 and under appears to be retarded by high incomes while high income stimulates out-migration of persons aged 65 and over.

Variables $X_{13}$ and $X_{16}$ are not expected to be related to migration patterns of younger persons, and for the most part they are not. The coefficient of $-.323$ (significant at the .05 level of confidence) for out-migration of this group and the proportion of persons aged 65 and over with incomes over $10,000 probably is a result of the association between post- and pre-retirement income.

*Migration Elasticities*

The conclusions emerging from examination of the migration elasticities in Table 6-6 are not nearly so clear-cut as those from the correlation coefficients contained in Tables 6-4 and 6-5. Most of the income elasticities which appear indicate results counter to our expectations, and represent changes from the results of Tables 6-4 and 6-5.

Our earlier arguments suggest that income should affect out-migration rates of elderly persons, but not their in-migration rates. Two of the four elasticities in Table 6-6 relating to migration of older persons, however, are for in-migration. Persons aged 65 and over and aged 65 to 69 apparently are attracted to states with high wages in the non-manufacturing sectors (variables $X_8$ and $X_9$).

---

[b]Obviously the most relevant of the three variables for younger persons is $X_{12}$. $X_{10}$ and $X_{11}$ exclude this group.

**Table 6-6**
**Migration-Rate Elasticities of Income Variables**

| Migration Rate | $X_7$ | $X_8$ | $X_9$ | $X_{12}$ | $X_{13}$ |
|---|---|---|---|---|---|
| Gross In-Migration | | | | | |
| Persons Aged 65+ | | | .97 | | |
| Persons Aged 65-69 | | 1.38 | | | |
| Persons Aged 64- | −.51 | .94* | | | −.41 |
| Gross Out-Migration | | | | | |
| Persons Aged 65+ | | | | | −.74* |
| Persons Aged 65-69 | | | | | −.73* |
| Persons Aged 64- | | | | −.84* | |

*Predicted sign.

**Wage Incomes.** The migration elasticity relating wages and in-migration of persons aged 65 and over can be explained if older persons do in fact migrate in response to wage opportunities. The group aged 65-69 should have more members just recently retired than the elderly group as a whole. Persons just recently retired may well have less interest in labor market participation (if the retirement were voluntary) than those retired for longer periods of time.[c]

**Total Incomes.** In the regression equations, the partial correlations between migration rates and variables $X_{14}$ and $X_{15}$ become insignificant. Thus while moderate levels of income are positively associated with migration, factors other than these moderate income levels are more important determinants of migration.

Negative out-migration elasticities appear for variable $X_{13}$ (proportion of older persons with incomes under $3,000) in both of the older groups. The coefficients of −.74 and −.73 indicate that low levels of income inhibit out-migration of all older persons, and of persons aged 65-69. This result is consistent with our predictions and is unchanged from the results achieved in the simple correlations in Table 6-5.

**Young Persons.** Elasticities in Table 6-6, contrary to the simple coefficients in Tables 6-4 and 6-5, suggest that younger persons migrate in response to wage and income signals that are similar to those affecting both elderly groups. A positive elasticity for in-migration accompanies variable $X_8$. Surprisingly, it is smaller than that for elderly persons (.94 vs. 1.38).

[c]The entry of $X_9$ for persons aged 65 and over and $X_8$ for those aged 65-69 probably has no special significance in terms of differences in behavior between the two groups. $X_8$ and $X_9$ are highly intercorrelated, so that if $X_8$ enters the step-wise regression program first, $X_9$ becomes insignificantly related to migration; if $X_9$ enters first, $X_8$ becomes insignificantly related to migration.

Another surprising result is the perverse influence of manufacturing wages (variable $X_7$) on migration of this age group. This may be explained by a high intercorrelation between past in-migration for the year 1949-1950 and current manufacturing wages. The presence of past migration in the equation causes the partial correlation of manufacturing wages and migration of younger persons to become negative. Current wages in FIRE and service industries are not so clearly related to past in-migration; hence, the presence of one of these variables with the expected sign in the final equation.

High incomes (variable $X_{12}$) are associated with low out-migration rates of younger persons. This result is consistent with the usual interpretation of migration theory. Interestingly, elasticities in Table 6-6 suggest that out-migration of older groups is retarded by low incomes, while that for younger persons is retarded by high incomes. Stated in another way, out-migration of older persons may be hindered more by low incomes than out-migration of younger persons. While this suggestion at first may seem questionable (especially since younger persons usually have larger families and ceteris paribus, their costs of moving will be greater), viewing migration in terms of human capital suggests that this result is reasonable. Younger persons, having a greater attachment to the labor force and greater expectations for high future earnings, could be expected to move from areas where their incomes are low to those where incomes are higher (and thus where migrants' expected incomes are higher) more readily than older persons. Having expectations of future higher incomes, they can finance their move more easily, and assume debt for the move more easily than older persons.

**Net Migration.** Wage and income variables are not very powerful in explaining net population movement. As indicated earlier, of course, it is difficult to isolate factors influencing net population movement. Only three elasticities appear (Table 6-7). The elasticities are positive and small, and consistent with elasticities of gross population movements appearing in Table 6-6.

**Table 6-7**
**Net Migration Elasticities for Wage and Income Variables[a]**

| Migration Rate | $X_9$ | $X_{14}$ | $X_{16}$ |
| --- | --- | --- | --- |
| Net Migration Persons Aged 65+ | .05 | .08 | |
| Net Migration Persons Aged 64- | | | .05* |

*Predicted sign.

[a]Only variables $X_9$, $X_{14}$, and $X_{16}$ are significant at the .05 level of confidence.

## Conclusions

As in other chapters, the simple correlations between the income variables and the various migration rates suggest stronger and more easily interpreted relationships between the two sets of variables than do the migration elasticities resulting from multiple regression equations. It was hypothesized that *in*-migration of elderly persons would not be influenced by income, but that incomes and *out*-migration of this age group would be positively associated. Younger persons were expected to migrate into states with high incomes and out of states with low incomes.

While the simple correlation coefficients are largely consistent with these hypotheses for both elderly and non-elderly persons, migration elasticities suggest that in-migration of elderly persons and incomes are positively related. Unchanged from the results of the simple correlation coefficients, is the suggestion that low incomes reduce out-migration of older persons, but stimulate out-migration of younger persons. These results suggest that younger persons' willingness and ability to migrate are determined largely by income potentials, while older persons' willingness and ability are determined largely by current incomes.

## Note

1. Larry A. Sjaastad, "The Relationship between Migration and Income in the United States," *Papers and Proceedings of the Regional Science Association* 6 (1960): 37-64.

# 7

## Labor-Force Behavior and Migration

The results we report in this chapter are at once our most promising and our most disappointing. We are convinced by our strongly felt intuitions and some meager empirical evidence that the process of disattachment from the labor force is a most important determinant of migration patterns of elderly persons. If this is true, forecasting migration patterns on the basis of information about characteristics of the labor force should be possible. Our statistical analysis has not verified this conjecture, but because of the apparent inconsistency of the results, cannot be said to have disproved it. The inconclusiveness of our findings is due mainly, we believe, to the hopeless mixing of cause and effect in the data we have employed. It is clear that full understanding and exploitation of the labor market attachment-migration nexus requires either more powerful statistical techniques or superior data, or both.

### Labor-Force Disattachment and Migration

In an earlier chapter we discussed some statistical evidence which suggests that retirement and migration decisions of elderly persons are closely associated. A simple choice-theoretic argument to explain this association can easily be constructed.

Locational choice can be thought of as an aspect of general consumer choice. Families purchase quantities of food, housing, clothing, but also hours of warm weather, hours on the beach, hours with friends and relatives, etc. The money prices and the relative prices of all these goods and services vary among residential locations. If a family's income were invariant with location, the family would simply choose that location whose prices allowed it to achieve the highest level of satisfaction. In technical terms, the family would choose that area in which the family's budget constraint was tangent to a higher indifference surface than could be reached in any other location.

Few persons can earn the same incomes in all locations. This is especially true of persons whose incomes are principally wages and salaries. This variability of earnings with respect to location causes the budget constraints to differ with location. When a person retires, this source of variability in the budget constraints is virtually eliminated. Social security payments, annuity income, rents, dividends, and interest can be received in any location, regardless of the location of the actual capital generating the income. Thus, the budget constraints a person faces in alternative locations shift when retirement occurs. It is to be expected, therefore, that some persons will find that their optimum residential locations at retirement differ from their optimum locations while working. For those persons for whom this is true, migration is the solution.

Our efforts to introduce these simple ideas into our statistical analysis have had two principal foci: (a) to measure the relationship between migration rates and various measures of labor force attachment of elderly persons, and (b) to discover characteristics of states which affect labor force attachment and thereby affect migration.

### Simple Correlation Coefficients

The variables used in pursuit of the first objective are unemployment rates, participation rates, weeks worked in one year, "special" participation rates, and turnover rates. These variables are:

$X_{17}$ = 1950-1960 average unemployment rate for males aged 65-69 in 1960

$X_{18}$ = 1950-1960 average unemployment rate for females aged 65-69 in 1960

$X_{19}$ = 1950-1960 average unemployment rate for persons aged 65-69 in 1960

$X_{20}$ = 1950-1960 average unemployment rate for the civilian labor force

$X_{21}$ = proportion of males aged 65+ who worked in 1959

$X_{22}$ = proportion of females aged 65+ who worked in 1959

$X_{23}$ = proportion of persons aged 65+ who worked in 1959

$X_{24}$ = proportion of males aged 65+ employed 1-13 weeks in 1959

$X_{25}$ = proportion of females aged 65+ employed 1-13 weeks in 1959

$X_{26}$ = proportion of persons aged 65+ employed 1-13 weeks in 1959

$X_{27}$ = proportion of males aged 65+ employed 14-39 weeks in 1959

$X_{28}$ = proportion of females aged 65+ employed 14-39 weeks in 1959

$X_{29}$ = proportion of persons aged 65+ employed 14-39 weeks in 1959

$X_{30}$ = proportion of males aged 65+ employed more than 39 weeks in 1959

$X_{31}$ = proportion of females aged 65+ employed more than 39 weeks in 1959

$X_{32}$ = proportion of persons aged 65+ employed more than 39 weeks in 1959

$X_{33}$ = 1959 labor-force turnover rate of males aged 65+

$X_{34}$ = 1959 labor-force turnover rate of females aged 65+

$X_{35}$ = 1959 labor-force turnover rate of persons aged 65+

Variables $X_{17}$ - $X_{20}$ measure unemployment rates, variables $X_{21}$ - $X_{23}$ measure labor force attachment, and variables $X_{24}$ - $X_{31}$, and $X_{33}$ - $X_{35}$ measure weeks worked per year and labor-force turnover rates, respectively.

Unfortunately, each of the labor force variables, measuring as they do labor force characteristics in 1959 and 1960, is itself affected by migration. We would much have preferred to measure these characteristics in 1955, but data with sufficient age detail were not available.

*Unemployment Rates*

Consider first the unemployment rates, variables $X_{17}$ - $X_{20}$. Table 7-1 contains average unemployment rates in all states for males, females and all persons aged 65-69 in 1960, and for the civilian labor force. Elderly males were experiencing the same unemployment rates—5 percent—as the civilian labor force, but because of the 3.8 percent unemployment rate of elderly females, the total unemployment rate for elderly persons was actually below that for the civilian force force as a whole. West Virginia's 9.3 percent unemployment rate for persons aged 65 and over was highest of all states, and the 3.6 percent unemployment

**Table 7-1**
**Selected Unemployment Rates, Average of 1950 and 1960**

| Variable | Unemployment Rate (Percentage) |
|---|---|
| Males Aged 65-69 | 5.0% |
| Females Aged 65-69 | 3.8 |
| Persons Aged 65-69 | 4.6 |
| Civilian Labor Force | 5.0 |

Source: U.S. Department of Commerce, Bureau of the Census, *1950 Census of Population*, Vol. II. *Characteristics of the Population* (Washington, D.C.: U.S. Government Printing Office, 1950), Table 66, and U.S. Department of Commerce, Bureau of the Census, *1960 Census of Population*, Vol. I, *Characteristics of the Population*. Part 1 (Washington, D.C.: U.S. Government Printing Office, 1960), Table 59, and ibid., Parts 2-52, Table 116.

rate in Iowa and North Carolina the lowest. Unemployment rates of elderly persons showed more variability among the states than those for the civilian labor force as a whole, as indicated by relative coefficients of variation for variables $X_{19}$ and $X_{20}$ of 35.4 and 23.8 respectively.

**Elderly Persons.** The simple correlation coefficients in Table 7-2 relating unemployment rates and migration indicate that states with higher unemployment rates for elderly males tended also to have higher rates of in-migration of the elderly, and vice versa. Clearly the migration rates must be interpreted as the causative factor, and the unemployment rates as the passive factor. On this interpretation, substantial numbers of elderly migrants must consider themselves to be members of the labor force but do not succeed in finding employment after migration.

Most of the coefficients of correlation relating unemployment rates to

**Table 7-2**
**Simple Correlation Coefficients Between 1950-1960 Unemployment Rates and Migration Rates**

| | Unemployment Rates | | | |
|---|---|---|---|---|
| Migration Rates | Males Aged 65+ in 1960 ($X_{17}$) | Females Aged 65+ in 1960 ($X_{18}$) | Persons Aged 65+ in 1960 ($X_{19}$) | Civilian Labor Force ($X_{20}$) |
| Gross In-Migration | | | | |
| Males Aged 65+ | .373[a] | .270 | .409 | .108 |
| Females Aged 65+ | .366 | .199 | .375 | .056 |
| Persons Aged 65+ | .376 | .238 | .397 | .081 |
| Males Aged 65-69 | .335 | .245 | .378 | .081 |
| Females Aged 65-69 | .369 | .215 | .384 | .034 |
| Persons Aged 65-69 | .355 | .233 | .384 | .058 |
| Persons Aged 64- | .246 | .117 | .242 | −.029 |
| Gross Out-Migration | | | | |
| Males Aged 65+ | .311 | .042 | .270 | .117 |
| Females Aged 65+ | .214 | −.054 | .167 | .100 |
| Persons Aged 65+ | .211 | −.071 | .177 | .114 |
| Males Aged 65-69 | .241 | −.051 | .191 | .141 |
| Females Aged 65-69 | .267 | .021 | .232 | .123 |
| Persons Aged 65-69 | .257 | −.012 | .215 | .133 |
| Persons Aged 64- | −.142 | −.221 | −.179 | .081 |

[a]Coefficients underlined once are significant at the .05 level of confidence; those underlined twice are significant at the .01 level of confidence.

out-migration also are positive, but not significant. Only that coefficient relating out-migration of males aged 65 and older to the unemployment rate of males aged 65-69 ($M_4$ to $X_{17}$) is significant at even the .05 level of confidence. Interpreting the migration rates as the causative factor, and unemployment at the passive factor, this generally positive (but not significant) association between out-migration of elderly persons and unemployment can be explained with the hypothesis that those elderly migrants who were members of the labor force before migration were also employed, so that their movement out of a state raises the state's unemployment rate.

These results together (positive associations between both in- and out-migration and unemployment) suggest, albeit very weakly, that elderly migrants who consider themselves to be members of the labor force are employed before migration but become unemployed after migration. This somewhat surprising possibility deserves greater attention in future research.

**Younger Persons.** Simple correlation coefficients in Table 7-2 indicate that younger persons are migrating in response to unemployment rates in a manner consistent with the usual model of migration; gross in-migration is negatively related, and gross out-migration is positively related, to unemployment rates. These coefficients, however, are not significant.

*Participation Rates*

Participation rates for all elderly males averaged 42.0 percent (Table 7-3), nearly three times greater than that for females. The average participation rates for all elderly persons in 1959 was 27.1 percent. Participation rates for this age group varied substantially among the 48 contiguous continental states; they were highest in Nevada and lowest in Louisiana (42.7 and 18.5 respectively).[a]

**Out-Migration.** Our statistical findings on participation rates are puzzling, to say the least. To see why, consider the following simple model:

let $M$ = number of elderly out-migrants from a state,

$N$ = number of employed elderly persons, and

$R$ = number of non-employed elderly persons.

Then $\dfrac{M}{N+R}$ = out-migration rate, and

---

[a]Florida is right behind Louisiana with a participation rate of 18.6 percent. Nevada's participation rate for males aged 65 and over was an amazing 63.7 percent, 12 percentage points above that in the next highest state.

**Table 7-3**
**Proportions of Persons Aged 65 and Over Who Worked in 1959**

|  | Participation Rate (percentage) |
|---|---|
| Males | 42.0% |
| Females | 14.3 |
| Total | 27.1 |

Source: U.S. Department of Commerce, Bureau of Census, *1960 Census of Population*, Vol. 1, *Characteristics of the Population* (Washington, D.C.: U.S. Government Printing Office, 1960), Table 118.

$$\frac{N}{N+R} = \text{participation rate.}$$

Assume that the probability of an employed person's migrating is $P_n$, and that the probability of a non-employed person's moving is $P_r$, and that non-employed persons are more likely to migrate than employed persons. Total out-migration is given by the statement

$$\frac{M}{N+R} = \frac{P_r R + P_n N}{N+R} = P_r \frac{R}{N+R} + P_n \frac{N}{N+R}$$

$$= P_r(1 - \frac{N}{N+R}) + P_n \frac{N}{N+R}$$

$$= P_r + (P_n - P_r) \frac{N}{N+R}.$$

The out-migration rate is seen to be a function of the participation rate. If the probability of migration of a person outside the labor force is greater than the probability of migration of a member of the labor force,[b] then this relationship between the out-migration rate and the participation rate is inverse. Examination of Table 7-4 reveals, however, that every correlation coefficient relating out-migration rates to participation rates (variables $X_{21}$ - $X_{23}$) is positive and significant at the .01 level of confidence.

To reconcile this finding with the simple model presented above, one could assume that the probability of migration is higher for employed persons than for

[b]Bowen and Finegan find such a relationship.[1]

**Table 7-4**

**Simple Correlation Coefficients between Participation Rates of Elderly Persons and Migration Rates**

| Migration Rates | Participation Rates | | |
|---|---|---|---|
| | Males $(X_{21})$ | Females $(X_{22})$ | Total $(X_{23})$ |
| Gross In-Migration | | | |
| Males Aged 65+ | −.195 | .115 | −.024 |
| Females Aged 65+ | −.099 | .185 | .071 |
| Persons Aged 65+ | −.143 | .153 | .024 |
| Males Aged 65-69 | −.225 | .073 | −.057 |
| Females Aged 65-69 | −.173 | .127 | −.009 |
| Persons Aged 65-69 | −.199 | .101 | −.032 |
| Gross Out-Migration | | | |
| Males Aged 65+ | .400[a] | .501 | .532 |
| Females Aged 65+ | .377 | .445 | .511 |
| Persons Aged 65+ | .442 | .529 | .588 |
| Males Aged 65-69 | .456 | .464 | .559 |
| Females Aged 65-69 | .483 | .553 | .623 |
| Persons Aged 65-69 | .475 | .520 | .601 |

[a]Coefficients underlined twice are significant at the .01 level of confidence.

persons not employed (retired, primarily). But this assumption appears to be at variance with the simple theoretical argument presented earlier in this chapter. It also cannot easily be reconciled with our findings in Chapter 1 that migration rates rise significantly above an otherwise steadily declining curve with respect to age at about the ages at which retirement typically occurs. Further, it is inconsistent with findings of other research.[2] Finally, this assumption violates our intuition concerning migration of elderly persons. We have been unable to construct any persuasive hypothesis to reconcile our theory, intuition, and disparate empirical results with respect to participation rates. This is a problem which could very well repay further investigation.

**In-Migration.** As was the case with unemployment rates, in-migration must be interpreted as the independent, and participation rates as the dependent, variable. With this interpretation and the assumption that persons outside the labor force are more likely to migrate than those in the labor force, in-migration and labor force participation should be negatively related. This inverse relationship would hold for migration rates of males $(X_{21})$, and for the majority of coefficients for all elderly persons $(X_{23})$, but none of the coefficients is significant. Furthermore, the coefficients for the female participation rates $(X_{22})$ are positive rather than negative. While they are not significant either, the difference *between* the coefficients for males and females *is*. This suggests that migration and participation rates are related in different ways for elderly males and elderly females. Further investigation of this phenomenon is indicated.

### *"Special" Participation Rates*

The distribution of the number of weeks worked during a year by elderly persons and the labor-force turnover rate indicates the strength of the labor-force attachment of elderly persons who worked at least one week in 1959.[c] High percentages of persons working less than 13 weeks a year and high turnover rates indicate a loose attachment; high percentages of persons working more than 39 weeks a year and low turnover rates indicate a tighter attachment to the labor force.

**National Averages.** Most elderly persons who worked in 1959 worked less than 3 months. Table 7-5 indicates that of all persons aged 65 and over who worked

**Table 7-5**
**Distribution of Employed Elderly Persons by Weeks Worked, 1959**

| Weeks Employed | Mean (Percentage) |
|---|---|
| 1-13 weeks | |
| Males | 65.7% |
| Females | 88.8 |
| Total | 78.1 |
| 14-39 weeks | |
| Males | 9.1 |
| Females | 3.8 |
| Total | 6.2 |
| more than 39 weeks | |
| Males | 25.2 |
| Females | 7.5 |
| Total | 15.7 |

Source: U.S. Department of Commerce, Bureau of Census, *1960 Census of the Population*, Vol. I, *Characteristics of the Population*, Parts 2-52 (Washington, D.C.: U.S. Government Printing Office, 1961), Table 118.

---

[c]Elderly persons in the labor force but unemployed all year do not enter into either of these sets of variables.

that year, over 78 percent worked 13 weeks or less. Interestingly, fewer worked 14 to 39 weeks than worked more than 39 weeks (6.2 percent vs. 15.7 percent). Females had a stronger tendency than males to work under three months, with 88.8 percent of them working this shorter period compared to 65.7 percent of the males.

**Variations Among States.** In Table 7-6, three of the four states identified as having exceptionally high percentages of older persons working 13 weeks are generally known as retirement states, with Nevada and Florida heading the list at 87.1 percent and 84.8 percent respectively. States with relatively high percentages of elderly persons working more than 39 weeks are interior states with important agricultural sectors. Nebraska heads this list at 20.8 percent.

States showing up in Table 7-7 as having the highest and lowest turnover rates do not follow our expectations. None of the states contained in Table 7-6 as having large percentages of older persons working 1-13 weeks or more than 39

**Table 7-6**
**States with Highest Percentages of Older Persons Working 1-13 Weeks and More than 39 Weeks, 1959**

| State | Percentage Working 1-13 Weeks | State | Percentage Working More Than 39 Weeks |
|---|---|---|---|
| Nevada | 87.1 | Nebraska | 20.8 |
| Florida | 84.8 | Wyoming | 20.3 |
| West Virginia | 83.2 | South Dakota | 20.2 |
| Arizona | 81.8 | Kansas | 18.7 |

Source: U.S. Department of Commerce, Bureau of Census, *1960 Census of the Population*, Vol. I *Characteristics of the Population*, Parts 2-52 (Washington, D.C.: U.S. Government Printing Office, 1961), Table 118.

**Table 7-7**
**States with Highest and Lowest Labor-Force Turnover Rates of Elderly Persons, 1959**

| High Turnover Rates (Column 1) | | Low Turnover Rates (Column 2) | |
|---|---|---|---|
| Mississippi | 1.62 | New Mexico | 1.30 |
| Maine | 1.60 | Montana | 1.31 |
| Arkansas | 1.59 | Delaware | 1.32 |

Source: U.S. Department of Commerce, Bureau of Census, *1960 Census of the Population*, Vol. I, *Characteristics of the Population* Parts 2-52 (Washington, D.C.: U.S. Government Printing Office, 1961), Tables 118 and 123.

weeks appears in Column 1 or Column 2 respectively. As it turns out, the frequency with which older persons enter and leave the labor force is unrelated to the tendency of these persons to work few or many weeks in any given year in which they are employed. The partial correlation coefficients between weeks worked in a year and the rate of labor-force turnover are not significant. This result suggests that labor-force turnover rates and weeks worked measure two separate aspects of labor-market behavior of elderly persons.

**Coefficients.** The correlation coefficients relating migration rates to the special participation rates ($X_{24}$ - $X_{32}$) are displayed in Table 7-8. The part-time (1-13 weeks of work per year) participation rates of males and persons ($X_{24}$ and $X_{26}$ respectively) are positively and significantly related to in-migration rates of all groups of elderly persons. This association suggests that the part-time participation rates of elderly migrants are generally higher than those of the population of the states into which they move, so that the migration tends to raise these rates for states with high in-migration rates. The relationships between out-migration rates and part-time participation are negative but generally not significant at the .05 confidence level.

"Intermediate-time" (14-39 weeks of work per year) participation rates ($X_{27}$ - $X_{29}$) generally have no significant association with in-migration rates. The positive association between persons working 14-39 weeks ($X_{29}$) and out-migration is puzzling. We can offer no explanation for this relationship at this time.

The full-time (more than 39 weeks of work per year) participation rates ($X_{30}$ - $X_{32}$) complement the part-time participation rates. The coefficients relating these variables to the in-migration rates are negative and mostly significant, while the coefficients for the out-migration rates are not significant. This suggests that the full-time participation rates of elderly migrants are lower than those of the elderly populations of the states into which they move.

*Turnover Rates*

Although these results concerning the special participation rates are, on the whole, fairly easily grasped, and somewhat informative regarding the employment characteristics of elderly migrants, as compared to non-migrants, they do not advance our understanding of the causes of migration, since our interpretations place migration in the role of causative, rather than caused, variable. The same can probably be said for the turnover rates. Most of the coefficients relating these rates to the migration rates are insignificant (Table 7-9). The few significant coefficients show inverse relationships between the turnover rates and out-migration rates. We interpret this to indicate that migrants are loosely attached to the labor force, so that states which lose large fractions of their

**Table 7-8**
**Simple Correlation Coefficients Between Number of Weeks Worked and Migration Rates of Elderly Persons**

| | Weeks Worked | | | | | | | | |
|---|---|---|---|---|---|---|---|---|---|
| | 1-13 Weeks | | | 14-39 Weeks | | | Over 39 Weeks | | |
| Migration Rates | Males $(X_{24})$ | Females $(X_{25})$ | Persons $(X_{26})$ | Males $(X_{27})$ | Females $(X_{28})$ | Persons $(X_{29})$ | Males $(X_{30})$ | Females $(X_{31})$ | Persons $(X_{32})$ |
| Gross In-Migration | | | | | | | | | |
| Males Aged 65+ | .493[a] | .071 | .347 | -.251 | .248 | .064 | -.573 | -.320 | -.477 |
| Females Aged 65+ | .395 | -.011 | .241 | -.219 | .241 | .087 | -.491 | -.231 | -.381 |
| Persons Aged 65+ | .445 | .026 | .294 | -.237 | .248 | .077 | -.534 | -.274 | -.430 |
| Males Aged 65-69 | .526 | .106 | .386 | -.307 | .224 | .017 | -.596 | -.351 | -.504 |
| Females Aged 65-69 | .456 | .033 | .314 | -.287 | .236 | .034 | -.533 | -.271 | -.434 |
| Persons Aged 65-69 | .494 | .073 | .352 | -.298 | .231 | .026 | -.568 | -.314 | -.472 |
| Gross Out-Migration | | | | | | | | | |
| Males Aged 65+ | -.091 | -.236 | -.237 | .237 | .148 | .322 | -.073 | .070 | .049 |
| Females Aged 65+ | -.109 | -.269 | -.272 | .226 | .188 | .356 | -.064 | .101 | .073 |
| Persons Aged 65+ | -.152 | -.274 | -.314 | .310 | .217 | .429 | -.046 | .088 | .089 |
| Males Aged 65-69 | -.165 | -.220 | -.293 | .268 | .062 | .291 | .008 | .104 | .119 |
| Females Aged 65-69 | -.095 | -.217 | -.248 | .336 | .206 | .439 | -.118 | .007 | .007 |
| Persons Aged 65-69 | -.132 | -.227 | -.276 | .309 | .144 | .377 | -.057 | .058 | .064 |

[a]Coefficients significant at the .01 level of confidence are underlined twice; those underlined once are significant at the .05 level of confidence.

**Table 7-9**

**Simple Correlation Coefficients between Labor-Force Turnover Rates of Elderly Persons and Migration Rates**

| | Turnover Rates | | |
|---|---|---|---|
| Migration Rates | Males ($X_{33}$) | Females ($X_{34}$) | Persons ($X_{35}$) |
| Gross In-Migration | | | |
| Males Aged 65+ | .201 | .002 | .097 |
| Females Aged 65+ | .157 | −.142 | −.034 |
| Persons Aged 65+ | .183 | −.072 | .032 |
| Males Aged 65-69 | .133 | −.004 | .060 |
| Females Aged 65-69 | .149 | −.094 | −.003 |
| Persons Aged 65-69 | .142 | −.049 | .029 |
| Gross Out-Migration | | | |
| Males Aged 65+ | .036 | −.397[a] | −.295 |
| Females Aged 65+ | .136 | −.478 | −.308 |
| Persons Aged 65+ | .100 | −.362 | −.231 |
| Males Aged 65-69 | .017 | −.483 | −.370 |
| Females Aged 65-69 | .103 | −.362 | −.230 |
| Persons Aged 65-69 | .065 | −.423 | −.298 |

[a]Coefficients underlined twice are significant at the .01 level of confidence, and those underlined once are significant at the .05 level of confidence.

elderly population through migration tend to have lower labor-force turnover rates. We cannot understand why the turnover rates are not, therefore, significantly correlated with in-migration rates. This is another conundrum which deserves further attention.

*Employment by Industry*

Our small efforts to discover variables which would enable us to forecast labor force attachment and thereby to forecast migration have been both unsuccessful and uninformative. Our approach to this matter has been to assume that the labor force attachment of elderly persons depends on the type of work they did when they were younger. For example, it could be that arduous physical labor simply requires retirement at moderately advanced age, while persons engaged in lighter work may retire later or not at all, or may remain employed on a part-time basis. In hopes of statistically capturing effects of this type, we have used as independent variables in our analysis the percentage distribution of employment by industry.[d] These variables are the 1950-1960 average proportion of the civilian labor force employed in:

$X_{36}$ = White-collar occupations

$X_{37}$ = Agriculture, forestry, and fisheries

$X_{38}$ = Mining

$X_{39}$ = Construction

$X_{40}$ = Durable goods manufacturing

$X_{41}$ = Non-durable goods manufacturing

$X_{42}$ = Communications and public utilities

$X_{43}$ = Wholesale and retail trade

$X_{44}$ = Finance, insurance, and real estate

$X_{45}$ = Business and repair services

$X_{46}$ = Personal services

$X_{47}$ = Entertainment and recreation services

$X_{48}$ = Professional and related services

$X_{49}$ = Public administration

$X_{50}$ = Industry not reported

Note that each of these variables is defined as the average percentage employed in a particular industry in the years 1950 and 1960.

Our view of the causal nexus between retirement and migration leads us to expect that the effects of industry of employment should be most visible in the correlations with out-migration rates. As Table 7-10 shows, the correlation coefficients for out-migration are generally larger (in absolute value) than the coefficients for in-migration. Even though a substantial number of the coefficients for both in- and out-migration are statistically significant, only one of these variables ($X_{38}$) has opposite signed coefficients for in- and out-migration, and these coefficients are not statistically significant.

The variables with the most disparate measured effects on in- and out-migration are construction employment ($X_{39}$), employment in business and repair services ($X_{45}$), and employment in personal services ($X_{46}$). In these three cases, the correlation coefficients are much larger for out-migration than for in-migration, and are all negative. But from the point of view of labor-force attachment these three types of employment are very dissimilar. Construction, of course, is

---

[d]Of course, the proportion of persons employed in white collar occupations ($X_{37}$) is not an industry, but an occupation variable. As such, it cuts across industry lines.

**Table 7-10**

**Simple Correlation Coefficients between Composition of Industry Employment and Migration Rates of Elderly Persons**

| | Gross In-Migration | | Gross Out-Migration | |
|---|---|---|---|---|
| Industry | Persons Aged 65+ ($M_3$) | Persons Aged 65-69 ($M_{12}$) | Persons Aged 65+ ($M_6$) | Persons Aged 65-69 ($M_{15}$) |
| $X_{36}$: White-collar Occupations | .233 | .237 | .217 | .296 |
| $X_{37}$: Agriculture, Forestries, Fisheries | −.342[a] | −.300 | −.475 | −.547 |
| $X_{38}$: Mining | −.046 | .000 | −.109 | −.102 |
| $X_{39}$: Construction | −.222 | −.149 | −.646 | −.642 |
| $X_{40}$: Durable Goods Mfg. | −.388 | −.343 | −.519 | −.457 |
| $X_{41}$: Non-Durable Goods Mfg. | −.498 | −.454 | −.712 | −.678 |
| $X_{42}$: Communications and Public Utilities | −.367 | −.304 | −.524 | −.482 |
| $X_{43}$: Wholesale and Retail Trade | −.384 | −.318 | −.625 | −.611 |
| $X_{44}$: Finance, Insurance and Real Estate | −.298 | −.234 | −.544 | −.522 |
| $X_{45}$: Business and Repair Services | −.279 | −.200 | −.704 | −.696 |
| $X_{46}$: Personal Services | −.156 | −.070 | −.697 | −.700 |
| $X_{47}$: Entertainment and Recreation Services | .122 | .099 | .175 | .203 |
| $X_{48}$: Professional and Related Services | .021 | .002 | .234 | .192 |
| $X_{49}$: Public Administration | .296 | .254 | .246 | .199 |
| $X_{50}$: Industry not Reported | −.204 | −.135 | −.543 | −.588 |

[a]Coefficients underlined once are significant at the .05 level of confidence; those underlined twice are significant at the .01 level of confidence.

hard, outdoor work (we recognize that the construction industry employs many white-collar workers), while service employment is light, indoor work. No reason can be seen why these three types of employment should especially discourage out-migration. Notice that for both elderly groups the only significant positive coefficients relate in-migration rates to percentage employed in public administration ($X_{49}$).

**Migration Elasticities**

Few of the labor force variables are significant in the multiple regression equations. Those that do enter do little to clear up interpretative difficulties encountered with the simple correlation coefficients. Our theoretical reasoning suggested that the effects of labor-force variables would be on out-migration, yet by far the majority of migration elasticities in the following tables are for in-migration. There is a strong possibility that states which attract elderly persons have characteristics closely associated with the labor-force participation and attachment variables employed by us which are not captured by other variables in the equations.

*Unemployment*

Contrary to the results of Table 7-2, in which in-migration of older persons and unemployment rates have high zero-order correlation coefficients, unemployment rates are insignificant in the multiple regression equations. The only unemployment rate that enters any of the equations is that for the labor force as a whole ($X_{20}$), and it enters only for one equation ($M_{15}$). It must be concluded that these results suggest that unemployment levels have little influence on migration decisions of elderly persons.

*Participation Rates*

Only one of the three participation rates (males aged 65 and above) is significantly related to migration in our multiple regression equations. Signs of all the elasticities are negative. Recall that we had suggested earlier that out-migration was a function of participation rates, and that a negative relationship between the two should exist. The negative signs for $X_{21}$ and out-migration in Table 7-11 are a change from those of the correlation coefficients (Table 7-4) and are one of the few results consistent with our hypotheses.

Negative elasticities for in-migration are explained best by reversing the dependent-independent roles of labor-force participation and migration. If elderly in-migrants have lower labor-force participation rates than elderly residents, in-migration will act to reduce the average participation rates and result in the observed negative association. This reversal of roles explains the

**Table 7-11**

**Migration Elasticities of Labor-Force Participation Rates of Elderly Persons**
$(X_{21} - X_{23})$

| Migration Rates | Participation Rate of Males Aged 65+ $(X_{21})$ |
|---|---|
| Gross In-Migration | |
| Males Aged 65+ | −1.13 |
| Persons Aged 65+ | −1.13 |
| Gross Out-Migration | |
| Females Aged 65-69 | −1.58* |
| Persons Aged 65-69 | −1.46* |

*Predicted sign.

signs of migration elasticities in in-migration equations for each of the labor-force variables.[e]

*"Special" Attachment Rates*

It was hypothesized earlier that elderly persons employed relatively few weeks during a year are more mobile than their counterparts who are employed longer periods in a year. This should result in positive associations between variables $X_{24} - X_{26}$ with out-migration. These expectations are not met. The only (isolated) elasticities in Table 7-12 for out-migration were for intermediate periods of work (variable $X_{29}$) for which no hypothesis was framed. In-migration equations contain elasticities for each of the three periods worked, with signs that are not even entirely consistent when migration is placed in the role of the independent variable.

Where the simple correlation coefficients relating labor-force turnover rates to in-migration are insignificant, migration elasticities are positive and significant for most of the in-migration equations (Table 7-13). It was hypothesized that turnover rates would be associated with out-migration rather than in-migration. The positive association between labor-force turnover rates and in-migration again places migration in the position of the independent variable.

[e]Interpretation of migration as the independent variable in this chapter indicates that the labor-force variables employed by us are not really appropriate for our equations. Our interest is to find factors that can be used to predict migration. But since migration undoubtedly has a strong impact on each of the labor force variables, we must know migration before we can determine the magnitude of these variables.

**Table 7-12**
**Migration Elasticities for Proportions of Elderly Persons Employed 1-13, 14-39, and over 39 Weeks**

| Migration Rate | Worked 1-13 Weeks | | Worked 14-39 Weeks[a] | | Worked over 39 Weeks |
| | Males | Females | Females | Persons | Persons |
| | $(X_{24})$ | $(X_{25})$ | $(X_{28})$ | $(X_{29})$ | $(X_{32})$ |
|---|---|---|---|---|---|
| Gross In-Migration | | | | | |
| Females Aged 65+ | | | −1.13 | 1.42 | |
| Persons Aged 65+ | | | − .51 | | |
| Males Aged 65-69 | 5.22 | | | | 1.06 |
| Females Aged 65-69 | | 4.31 | | | |
| Gross Out-Migration | | | | | |
| Females Aged 65-69 | | | | .65 | |
| Persons Aged 65-69 | | | | .74 | |

[a]No sign was hypothesized.

**Table 7-13**
**Migration Elasticities of Labor-Force Turnover Rates of Elderly Persons $(X_{33} - X_{35})$**

| Migration Rate | Females $(X_{34})$ | Persons $(X_{35})$ |
|---|---|---|
| Gross In-Migration | | |
| $M_1$: Males Aged 65+ | | 3.11 |
| $M_3$: Persons Aged 65+ | | 2.86 |
| $M_{10}$: Males Aged 65-69 | 2.10 | |
| $M_{11}$: Females Aged 65-69 | 2.03 | |
| $M_{12}$: Persons Aged 65-69 | | 1.98 |

*Employment by Industry*

Migration elasticities contained in Table 7-14 for employment by industry are a little more intelligible than the simple correlation coefficients for these same variables. States with relatively large proportions of persons employed in agriculture $(X_{37})$ and entertainment and recreation services $(X_{47})$ appear to attract elderly persons, while those with large public sectors $(X_{49})$ appear to discourage in-migration of these persons. States with large proportions of persons employed in white-collar occupations $(X_{36})$, construction $(X_{39})$, non-durable goods manufacturing $(X_{41})$, and personal services $(X_{46})$ may experience

**Table 7-14**
**Migration Elasticities of Employment by Industry ($X_{37}$ - $X_{50}$)**

| Migration Rates | $X_{37}$ | $X_{38}$ | $X_{40}$ | Industry Variables $X_{42}$ | $X_{43}$ | $X_{47}$ | $X_{48}$ | $X_{50}$ |
|---|---|---|---|---|---|---|---|---|
| Gross In-Migration | | | | | | | | |
| Males Aged 65+ | | | | | | | | −.07 |
| Males Aged 65-69 | | | | | | | .05 | |
| Females Aged 65-69 | | .17 | | | | | .05 | −.05 |
| Gross Out-Migration | | | | | | | | |
| Females Aged 65+ | | | | | | −.14* | | |
| Persons Aged 65+ | −.68* | | | −.13* | | | | |
| Females Aged 65-69 | | | | | | | .08 | |
| Persons Aged 65-69 | | | −.44 | | .49 | | | |

*Predicted sign.

lower out-migration rates of elderly persons. The positive elasticities for out-migration and $X_{42}$ and $X_{47}$ are contrary to our hypotheses, as are the negative elasticities previously mentioned for construction and non-durable goods manufacturing.

## Conclusions

Of the variables discussed in this chapter, the only one with consistently significant coefficients in the multiple regression equations is the level of the elderly participation rate of males $(X_{21})$.

While the signs of the simple coefficients between $X_{21}$ and out-migration were opposite those expected, those in the out-migration elasticities were negative as hypothesized. Our uncertainty about the direction of the cause and effect, and the difficulties this poses for interpreting statistical results, however, makes it difficult for us to reach any conclusions regarding these findings.

Unemployment rates, the other participation rates (including the "special participation rates") enter only very rarely in scattered places in the tables of regression coefficients. This indicates that holding other variables constant renders the influence of these variables on migration generally insignificant. The turnover rate for females does enter all the in-migration equations for persons aged 65-69. The only industrial composition variables to appear more than twice in the migration elasticity equations are the percentage of the labor force employed in entertainment and recreation services.

Migration of elderly persons clearly seems to be related to labor-force participation and turnover rates, but the statistical interpretation of this association is problematical. It probably would be better to pursue research designed to investigate the influence of migration on these variables rather than the other way around, as we have attempted to do here.

## Notes

1. William G. Bowen and T. Aldrich Finegan, *The Economics of Labor Force Participation* (Princeton, N.J.: Princeton University Press, 1969).
2. Ibid.

# 8

## Miscellaneous Factors and Migration

### Introduction

In this chapter we deal with the possible effects of several miscellaneous factors on the migration rates of elderly persons. These factors are:

1. relative population of contiguous states,
2. education,
3. housing market conditions,
4. geography (North vs. South), and
5. availability of entertainment and recreation services.

We depart here from the usual organization of these chapters. In each section below we discuss one of the miscellaneous factors. Within each section we deal with our a priori reasoning concerning the effect of that factor, the variable(s) used to measure the influence of the factor, our expectations concerning the signs of the correlation coefficients and elasticities, and the actual results. Conclusions are summarized below.

### Relative Population

Simple correlation coefficients suggest that out-migration from a state is strongly associated with the relative size of populations in surrounding states. This association disappears, however, in the multiple regression equations.

### Education

As with relative population, education appears to influence strongly migration when simple correlation coefficients are examined, but its direct influence[a] disappears when migration elasticities are calculated.

### Housing Market Conditions

Occupancy and rental rates are seen to exert influence on migration of all age groups. Migration elasticities of occupancy rates are consistently larger than those of any other variable.

---

[a]Education may well operate indirectly through income and past migration experiences, variables which have been examined in previous chapters.

*Geography*

Migration out of southern states is lower than that out of northern states, but the nature of the variable utilized conceals much of the expected relationship between geography and in-migration.

*Entertainment and Recreation Services*

Except for the age group 65-69, little association is found between the availability of entertainment and recreation services and migration.

## Relative Populations in Contiguous States

*Gravity Hypotheses*

"Gravity" models of migration suggest that population attracts population. That is, population is said to be analogous to mass, so that large concentrations of population exert a strong gravitational attraction on population in other areas, while small concentrations of population exert only a small attractive force. As in the physical gravity model, this attractive force is assumed to vary inversely with the square of the distance between the attracting mass of population and the potential migrant.

*Population Variable*

While such models of the migration process appear to have weak theoretical foundations, they have been somewhat successful in explaining migration patterns. Unfortunately, our migration data are not adequate for full-blown testing of the gravity concepts in relation to migration of the elderly. Since we have no information concerning place-to-place flows of migrants, it is impossible for us to test rigorously whether the attractive force of population concentrations varies in the usual way with distance.

We have, however, formulated a simple hypothesis which is closely related to the gravity theories. The hypothesis is that states which are relatively small (in population) compared to their immediate neighbors (contiguous states) would experience greater out-migration rates than states which are relatively large compared to their neighbors. To test this hypothesis we have employed the following variables:

$X_{4,i}$ = Sum of the population (all ages of all states contiguous to state $i$)/population (all ages) of state $i$;

$X_{5,i}$ = Sum of the populations (aged 65 and older) of all states contiguous to state $i$/population (65 and older) of state $i$;

$X_{6,i}$ = Sum of populations (aged 64 and younger) of all states contiguous to state $i$/population (aged 64 and younger) of state $i$.

*Empirical Data*

As might be expected, states with small elderly population relative to their neighbors generally are interior states, and those with large elderly populations relative to their neighbors are "border" states. The ratio of the number of elderly persons living in states contiguous to Nevada to the number of elderly persons living in Nevada—97.4—was the highest in the nation in 1960. Delaware (53.6), Vermont (53.2), and New Mexico (27.4) followed. States having large elderly populations relative to their neighbors are California (.2), Maine (.6), Washington (.9), and Texas (1.0). With the exception of New Mexico, these respective eight states also have the smallest and the largest total populations (and populations aged 64 and under) relative to states contiguous to them.

Table 8-1 contains the means and standard deviations of the three contiguous population variables. They indicate that about ten times as many persons lived in states surrounding any given state than lived in that state, and that there is little difference in this pattern between young and old persons. The standard deviation of the variable for older persons, however, is larger than that for younger persons, suggesting, as other data have, that elderly persons are more unevenly distributed among the states than are younger persons.

**Table 8-1**
**Ratio of Population in Contiguous States to Population in Individual States, 1960**

| Population Groups | Mean | Standard Deviation |
|---|---|---|
| All Persons | 9.78 | 13.74 |
| Persons Aged 65+ | 10.80 | 16.77 |
| Persons Aged 64- | 9.72 | 13.57 |

Source: Calculated from U.S. Department of Commerce, Bureau of the Census, *1960 Census of Population*, Vol. I, *Characteristics of the Population*, Part 1, United States Summary (Washington, D.C.: U.S. Government Printing Office, 1961), Table 59.

*Predicted Signs*

We expected the contiguous population variables to be positively associated with out-migration rates of both elderly and non-elderly persons. This association should be especially high between $X_5$ and the migration variables relating to older persons, and between $X_6$ and the migration variables relating to younger persons. Variable $X_4$ may not be related closely to either group.

*Simple Correlation Coefficients*

Simple correlation coefficients in Table 8-2 appear to support the "gravity" theory. Every gross out-migration rate is positively associated with each of the contiguous population variables (including those for males and females taken individually) at the .01 level of significance. Coefficients relating the contiguous population variables with in-migration are significant at the .05 confidence level only for persons under age 64 (Table 8-2) and for females aged 65 and older (not shown). The positive coefficients for the in-migration variables can be rationalized on the ground that states with relatively small populations compared to their neighbors are surrounded by a large pool of potential migrants. Relatively low migration rates out of the surrounding states could result in relatively high migration into the "surrounded" states.

*Migration Elasticities*

Table 8-3 contains every migration variable for which any of the contiguous population variables is significant. The table reveals that the contiguous population variables are generally significant in explaining out-migration rates of elderly

**Table 8-2**
**Simple Correlation Coefficients between the Contiguous Population Variables and Migration Rates**

| Migration Rate | All Ages $X_4$ | Aged 65+ $X_5$ | Aged 64- $X_6$ |
|---|---|---|---|
| Gross In-Migration | | | |
| Persons Aged 65+ | .259 | .256 | .260 |
| Persons Aged 65-69 | .224 | .223 | .225 |
| Persons Aged 64- | .316[a] | .333 | .315 |
| Gross Out-Migration | | | |
| Persons Aged 65+ | .543* | .543* | .542* |
| Persons Aged 65-69 | .527* | .534* | .526* |
| Persons Aged 64- | .619* | .612* | .620* |
| *Expected sign. | | | |

[a]Coefficients underscored once are significant at .05 level of confidence; those underscored twice are significant at .01 level of confidence.

**Table 8-3**
**Migration-Rate Elasticities of Contiguous Population Variables**

| Migration Rate | Aged 65+ $X_5$ | Aged 64- $X_6$ |
|---|---|---|
| Gross In-Migration | | |
| All Persons Aged 65+ | .08 | |
| Gross Out-Migration | | |
| Males Aged 65+ | | .15* |
| Females Aged 65+ | | .08* |
| Males Aged 65-69 | .12* | |
| Females Aged 65-69 | .13* | |
| All Persons Aged 65-69 | .16* | |
| Females Aged 64- | .07* | |

*Predicted sign.

persons when the influence of other variables is taken into account. These variables, however, appear in only one of the equations for out-migration rates of younger persons. They appear in one in-migration equation for older persons. We have framed no formal hypothesis concerning a relationship between relative populations in contiguous states and in-migration. Thus it is not clear how the .08 coefficient between in-migration of males aged 65 through 69 and relative populations of elderly persons should be viewed.

*Conclusions*

Both the correlation coefficients and the migration elasticities lend support to our weak version of the gravity hypothesis for elderly persons. Younger persons appear not to be attracted by nearby populations, if other factors are held constant, although the simple correlations do suggest such an attraction.[b]

**Education**

The possible effects of education on mobility are subtle, complex, and intertwined with other factors, especially income. One would suppose that

[b]It should be pointed out that the gravity models suffer from some of the same difficulties of interpretation as do those relating migration in different periods. It is not clear whether elderly persons are moving away from places with relatively small elderly populations to those with relatively large elderly populations simply because of the relative population sizes or because the same things that attracted elderly persons in the past are still attracting elderly persons in the present.

educated persons read more widely than uneducated persons. Consequently they should be more aware of the rest of the country and of the advantages of different locations in comparison with their current locations. Furthermore, persons with college educations often live away from home while attending college, so that their awareness is increased directly, and their attachments to home are reduced. These effects on migration rates of elderly persons are likely to be somewhat complex, however, since the level of education of any given person is established fairly early in life (say, before age 25).

This means that the largest effects of education level on mobility are likely to be felt in the years before retirement. Therefore, the mobility of retired persons could be affected by their educational levels indirectly through the effects on their prior histories of migration, effects previously discussed in Chapter 4 and separately accounted for in our statistical analysis. Another complicating factor is that education and income are highly correlated. The result is that education levels also affect mobility rates indirectly through their effects on income levels which affect mobility; these effects have been discussed in Chapter 6.

*Empirical Data*

Unfortunately, aggregative education-level statistics by state and age are not available. Consequently, the variable we have used to represent education level in our statistical analysis is

$X_{51}$ = Median number of years of formal education of the population, aged 25 and older, 1950-1960 average.

This variable overestimates the education level of elderly persons, since the amount of formal education received in the United States has been rising over time. We can only hope, however, that the degree of overestimation is roughly the same for all states.

The average education level in the United States between 1950 and 1960 was 10.0 years. Utah had the "most educated" population at 12.1 years, and was the only state with an average above 12 years. Lowest was Louisiana, in which residents had completed an average of 8.2 years of schooling. The southern and southeastern states generally had the lowest averages; states in the West and Far West had the highest.

*Predicted Signs*

The a priori points made earlier suggest that years of education should be positively associated with out-migration rates, but not significantly associated with in-migration rates. However, our simple statistical techniques present problems. If it is true that larger percentages of highly educated persons move upon retirement than of less educated persons, the states out of which they move have the median education level lowered by the movement; likewise, the states into which they move have the median education level raised. This suggests that positive association between in-migration rates and education levels might be observed. This same phenomenon would have the effect of reducing the association between out-migration rates and education, even possibly rendering the correlation negative.

## Simple Correlation Coefficients

**Older Persons.** Examination of the simple correlation coefficients in Table 8-4 reveals that the association between education level and out-migration rates is indeed positive and highly significant for elderly persons (the coefficients exceed .5 for persons 65 and older and for persons 65-69). The correlation between education level and *in*-migration rates, however, also is positive, as suggested might be the case by the argument in the preceding paragraph. These simple coefficients are all significant at least at the .05 confidence level. However, they are considerably smaller than the coefficients for out-migration rates. We interpret these results as at least weak confirmation of the hypothesis that highly educated elderly persons are more likely to move than less-educated elderly persons.

**Table 8-4**
**Association between Education and Migration**

| Migration Rate | Simple Correlation Coefficient | Migration Elasticity |
|---|---|---|
| Gross In-Migration | | |
| Persons Aged 65+ | .418[a] | – |
| Persons Aged 65-69 | .386 | – |
| Persons Aged 64- | .484 | – |
| Gross Out-Migration | | |
| Persons Aged 65+ | .534* | – |
| Persons Aged 65-69 | .590* | – |
| Persons Aged 64- | .201 | – |

*Predicted sign.

[a]Coefficients underlined twice are significant at .01 level of significance.

**Younger Persons.** The simple correlation coefficients for migration rates of non-elderly persons in Table 8-4 suggest that if education does influence migration, the principal effect of education on migration may act indirectly through income levels. The coefficients are positive for both in- and out-migration rates (.484 and .201 respectively), but those for out-migration rates are not significant at the .05 confidence level. This is what one would expect if (and this is certainly true) high education-level states are also high income-level states. As we showed in Chapter 6, younger persons are definitely attracted to high income states—much more so than elderly persons.

*Migration Elasticities*

Once again, results from the multiple regression equations differ substantially from those suggested by simple correlation coefficients. The education variable does not appear in *any* of the gross migration equations. This is true for equations by sex as well as for those by the population totals contained in Table 8-4. Education does appear four times in net migration equations, and these isolated entries have signs opposite those predicted.

**Relation to Other Variables.** Examination of intermediate steps in the regression program reveals that when past in-migration (variable $X_1$) discussed in Chapter 4 enters an in-migration equation, the partial correlation of education with migration becomes insignificant. This is true for every age category included in the study. Education level disappears most often from the out-migration equations for elderly persons when out-migration ($X_2$) and proportion of employment in personal services ($X_{46}$) enter the equations, and from the gross out-migration equations of younger persons when proportion of employment in white-collar occupations ($X_{36}$) enters. In some of the equations, education level enters early, decreases gradually in significance as other variables enter, and becomes insignificant only after six or seven other variables have been taken into account. This intercorrelation among the variables may account for the absence of education in the migration elasticities.

*Conclusions*

Simple correlation coefficients suggest that education and out-migration of elderly persons are closely and positively related as predicted. As expected, this positive association also holds for in-migration. Correlations between out-migration and younger persons are positive but not significant. While education is not significant in the regression equations, the non-significance probably results from the influence of education working through other variables. It seems to be kept out of the in-migration equations because of its close association with past in-migration rates, and out of the out-migration equations by its association with a number of variables (including past out-migration).

## Housing

Just as employment and educational opportunities might loom relatively large in locational decision of families with heads aged, say, 25-50, health care and housing might loom relatively large in locational decision of elderly persons. Health care has been discussed in Chapter 5. Two aspects of housing market conditions—availability and costs—are examined here.

### Occupancy Rates

The variable selected to represent the availability of housing is occupancy rates. While all empty units will not be suitable for occupancy by elderly persons, we assume that there is some regular relationship between the total number of vacant units and the number of vacant units which are potential housing for older persons. High occupancy rates are expected to discourage in-migration, and act in an opposite fashion for out-migration.

### Housing Costs

It would have been good to be able to utilize statewide cost-of-living indexes rather than housing costs to measure relative living expenses, but published indexes cover SMSAs rather than states. The Retired Couple's Budget published by the Bureau of Labor Statistics would serve as an estimate of living costs, but not all states are represented in that index.

**Median Rents.** In the absence of a complete index, we selected the median rent in occupied housing units to represent the overall cost of living. Since the degree to which any particular price should affect migration probably depends on the importance of the product or service in the budget, prices of items which comprise a substantial part of the budget should have powerful effects on mobility rates. This argument suggests that the cost of housing should be particularly significant in influencing migration rates of the elderly.

**Expected Signs.** Rental levels should affect the migration decision of an elderly family in rather obvious ways. High rents should encourage out-migration and discourage in-migration, while low rents should have the opposite effects.

Consider an elderly family contemplating migration from an area with high rental rates. If the family is currently renting, the high-rental rates should raise the probability of migration. If the family owns its own house then the high-rental rates will be reflected in the value of that house, so that a substantial sum of money can be realized from the sale of the house; this sum of money could then be used to finance the migration. If the family decides to move, the cost of housing should also influence its destination. By moving away from the high-rental state to a low-rental state the family frees some of its income for the purchase of goods and services other than housing. If the family sells a house in the current location and buys a less costly house in the new location, then part of the family's wealth is converted from relatively illiquid form to more liquid form, so that additional consumption of other goods and services can be financed without reducing the quality of housing consumed.

### Definition of Variables

The two variables we use to represent housing conditions and cost of living are:

$X_{52}$ = Proportion of housing units occupied, 1950-1960 average;

$X_{53}$ = Median monthly rent in occupied housing units, 1950-1960 average.

### Empirical Data

Means, standard deviations, and coefficients of variation for $X_{52}$ and $X_{53}$ are contained in Table 8-5. The average proportion of occupied housing is .91. Illinois had the highest occupancy rate at .95 and Maine the lowest at .79. The highest average rental rates were in Nevada at $69.15 a month; lowest were in Mississippi ($33.80), less than half the rates in Nevada. The relatively large coefficient of variation for rental rates indicated that housing costs varied more among states than did amounts of available housing.[c]

### Simple Correlation Coefficients

We anticipated that both rental and occupancy rates would be directly related to out-migration rates and inversely related to in-migration rates. The simple correlation coefficients in Table 8-6 do not strongly confirm these hypotheses, but the results are favorable.

[c]This is expected, since housing costs reflect difference in quality of housing and in states' dependence on property taxes, as well as differences in availability.

**Table 8-5**
**Occupancy and Median Rental Rates, 1950-1960 Average**

| Variable | Mean | Standard Deviation | Coefficient of Variation |
|---|---|---|---|
| Proportion of Housing Units Occupied | .91 | .03 | 3.90 |
| Median Monthly Rent | $52.85 | 8.58 | 16.23 |

Source: U.S. Department of Commerce, Bureau of the Census, *County and City Data Book* (Washington, D.C.: U.S. Government Printing Office, 1956), Table II, and 1962, Table II.

**Table 8-6**
**Simple Correlation Coefficients between Housing Variables and Migration**

| Migration Rate | Occupancy Rate | Rental Rate |
|---|---|---|
| Gross In-Migration | | |
| Persons Aged 65+ | −.467*a | .249 |
| Persons Aged 65-69 | −.434* | .213 |
| Persons Aged 64- | −.342* | .232 |
| Gross Out-Migration | | |
| Persons Aged 65+ | −.268 | .556* |
| Persons Aged 65-69 | −.215 | .562* |
| Persons Aged 64- | −.221 | −.101 |

*Expected sign.

aCoefficients underlined once (twice) are significant at the .05 (.01) level of confidence.

**Occupancy Rate.** Occupancy rate is highly (significant at the .01 confidence level) and inversely related to in-migration rates of persons 65 and older and of persons 65-69, as hypothesized. Contrary to our expectations, the relationship between occupancy rate and out-migration rates of these groups is also inverse; however, the coefficients are not significant at the .05 level. The same comments hold for the migration rates of non-elderly persons, except that the coefficient relating the occupancy rate to in-migration is significant at only the .05 confidence level.

**Rental Rates.** The simple correlation coefficients for the rental variable also confirm our hypotheses. The relationships between rental level and out-migration are highly significant and positive for persons 65 and older and for persons 65-69, as we anticipated. The relationships between rental levels and in-migration rates are also positive, contrary to our expectations, but they are not significant. Surprisingly, rental rates are negatively associated with out-migration of younger persons.

*Migration Elasticities*

Rental rates $(X_{53})$ appear in two out-migration equations, with the expected signs, and in one in-migration equation with the wrong sign. It is worth noting that the out-migration elasticities relate to elderly females only. Thus while weak support for our hypothesis regarding the effect of rental rates on out-migration of older persons, such support as we find relates to the group most likely to be sensitive to this variable—females.

Occupancy rates maintain their significance when we consider the complete equations. In-migration coefficients are negative as predicted, and unusually large. A 1 percent variation in the occupancy rate is associated with a variation in the in-migration rates of persons over age 64 by approximately 2 percent, a variation of in-migration rates of persons aged 65-69 by 4.5 percent, and a variation of in-migration rates of younger males by more than 1 percent. Overall, these are the largest elasticities we encountered throughout the study.

The elasticities in Table 8-7 suggest that, holding other things constant, high

**Table 8-7**
**Migration-Rate Elasticities of Housing Variables**

| Migration Rate | Occupancy Rate | Rental Rate |
|---|---|---|
| Gross In-Migration | | |
| Males Aged 65+ | −3.84* | |
| Females Aged 65+ | −2.62* | |
| Persons Aged 65+ | −2.01* | |
| Males Aged 65-69 | −5.28* | |
| Females Aged 65-69 | −3.33* | |
| Persons Aged 65-69 | −4.52* | 1.27 |
| Males Aged 64- | −1.25* | |
| Gross Out-Migration | | |
| Females Aged 65+ | | 1.28* |
| Females Aged 65-69 | | 1.05* |
| Net Migration | | |
| Males Aged 65+ | −.22* | |
| Persons Aged 64- | −.22* | |

*Predicted sign.

occupancy rates strongly discourage in-migration, but they do not significantly affect out-migration, as suggested by the simple correlation coefficients. The following explanation of this phenomenon appears plausible. The average occupancy rate in a given location is not a relevant matter to a person who has a place to live. If a person does not have a place to live he could not be counted as a resident of that location in the census. Once a person has decided to move, however, the average occupancy rate in potential new locations is relevant information. He would be less certain of being able to find a suitable place to live in areas with very high occupancy rates.

**Younger Persons.** Note that younger persons are less sensitive to occupancy rates than older persons. Younger persons' in-migration is reduced by less than half as much by declining vacancies than all older persons, and only a third as much as persons aged 65-69. This can be explained if younger persons are drawn to an area primarily because of a (potential) job while older persons are drawn primarily because an area "might be a nice place to live." If this is the case, younger persons probably will be less concerned about the ready availability of housing than older persons. The same result can be explained if more young persons move to an area planning to build their own homes. In this case, the higher incomes of persons under 65 permit them to move more readily to areas with housing shortages; the influence of greater labor-force attachment is there, but operating indirectly through income rather than directly through the relative importance of housing in the decision to move.

*Conclusions*

We predicted that high occupancy and rental rates would discourage in-migration and encourage out-migration of elderly persons. Our findings suggest that high occupancy rates do in fact have a strong negative effect on in-migration of all elderly subgroups. The simple inverse-causation arguments discussed in Chapter 7 cannot account for the strong results. High in-migration should, ceteris paribus, *raise* occupancy rates. Yet our results show an inverse relationship. One could argue, however, that rapid population growth stimulates local construction industries to "build ahead of demand," thereby reducing occupancy rates. Running counter to our expectations, but understandable once the results are considered, is the lack of impact of occupancy rates on out-migration. Once we recognize that residents in an area will have housing regardless of how high the current occupancy rate may be, it is clear that high occupancy rates alone might not induce out-migration.

Given the previously-discussed multicollinearity among variables $X_{13}$, $X_{53}$, and $X_{54}$, the absence of $X_{53}$ in the migration equations is not indicative of the actual impact of rental rates on migration decisions of the elderly. The simple correlations between $X_{53}$ and out-migration of persons aged 65 and over are indeed positive and highly significant. Furthermore, rental rates do enter migration equations for elderly females, and suggest that high rents increase net out-migration of these persons. We conclude that rental rates do influence migration of elderly persons in the manner predicted.

Migration decisions of persons under age 65 are influenced by occupancy in about the same fashion as are those of older persons, but the elasticities are lower for the former group. In-migration rates are reduced by high occupancy rates, but neither in- nor out-migration is affected by rental rates.

## Geographical Location

States differ with respect to a number of physical characteristics which variously attract and repel different groups of potential migrants. Some such characteristics are rainfall, temperature, presence or absence of bodies of water suitable for water-based recreation, presence or absence of mountainous terrain, and humidity. These characteristics pose substantial measurement problems. Most states have a diversity of physical characteristics—areas with high, and areas with low rainfall; areas with cool, and areas with moderate climates, etc. Consequently, characterizing any one state as being, for example, mountainous, cool, and wet probably will not reflect conditions prevailing in the entire state.

### North versus South

Possibly the single most important physical characteristic of states in affecting migration is temperature (a characteristic actually reflecting influences of several others mentioned above). The simplest way to represent temperature as a variable, and the way we have chosen, is to divide the country into two climatic regions. The selected variable is of the dichotomous type, defined as follows:

$$X_{54,i} = \begin{cases} 1, \text{ if the majority of the land area of state } i \text{ lies north of the 37th} \\ \quad \text{parallel} \\ 2, \text{ if the majority of the land area of state } i \text{ lies south of the 37th} \\ \quad \text{parallel.}^{d} \end{cases}$$

Figure 8-1 shows which states fall north, and which fall south, of this parallel. California is the only state for which we had to make an arbitrary decision

---

[d]The 1,2 dichotomy, rather than the more familiar 0,1 dichotomy, is used because in the statistical analysis we perform logarithmic transformations of all the variables. The $s$ transformation cannot be performed for a 0,1 variable because the logarithm of zero is not defined.

115

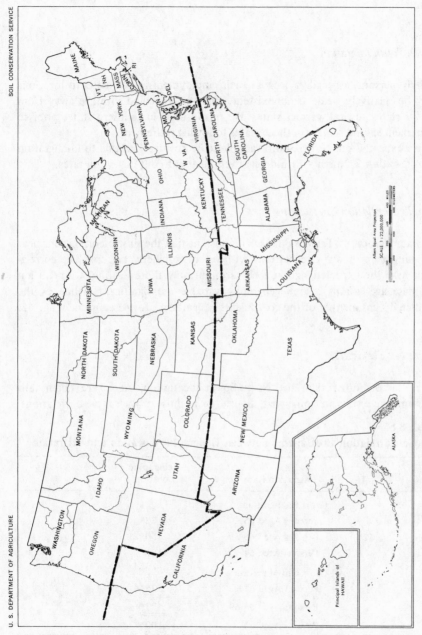

**Figure 8-1.** Classification of States by "North" and "South".

concerning the North-South classification. California is classified as "South" since the major concentrations of population are in the southern part of the state.

## North-South Migration

Elderly persons, especially, because their employment attachments to locations may be relatively weak or nonexistent, might be expected to move away from colder states toward warmer states. Persons residing in southern states prior to retirement should remain in those states following retirement.

We expected our North-South variable to be positively related to in-migration rates (South = 2, North = 1) and negatively related to out-migration rates.

## Simple Correlation Coefficients

An examination of Table 8-8 makes it apparent that the simple correlations bear out only part of our expectations with regard to elderly persons. The correlations have the expected sign in each case, but only those relating out-migration of these age groups to the geography variable are significant. While of the predicted signs, neither of the coefficients is significant for persons under age 65.

## Migration Elasticities

When factors other than the North-South location of states are taken into account, the results are somewhat changed from those of the simple correlations.

**Table 8-8**
**Simple Correlation Coefficients between Geographic Location and Migration**

| Migration Rate | Geographic Location |
|---|---|
| Gross In-Migration | |
| Persons Aged 65+ | .172* |
| Persons Aged 65-69 | .250* |
| Persons Aged 64- | .131* |
| Gross Out-Migration | |
| Persons Aged 65+ | −.525*a |
| Persons Aged 65-69 | −.575* |
| Persons Aged 64- | −.100* |

*Predicted sign.
[a]Coefficients underlined twice are significant at the .01 level of confidence.

**Elderly Persons.** For persons 65 and older the previously noted tendency of southern states to experience lower out-migration than northern states appears. For persons aged 65-69, however, both in- and out-migration rates of males are significantly related to geography (in one case for males, in the other, for females); in-migration rates are higher, and out-migration rates lower for southern states.

**Younger Persons.** The North-South variable $(X_{54})$ enters the regression equations identified in Table 8-9 even though there was no significant simple relationship (as seen in Table 8-8) between $X_{54}$ and migration of younger persons. Southern states experience lower out-migration rates of both males and females aged 64 and below than do northern states. This age group, which we expected to be less sensitive to geography variations than older persons, is the only age group for which geography acts in a consistent manner for both males and females in the out-migration equations, and the migration elasticities are as large or larger (when they enter) than those for older persons.

### Conclusions

Contrary to our expectations, and contrary to the visual presentation of broad migration patterns of older persons earlier in the book, our formal statistical tests reveal no consistent in-migration of elderly persons into the southern states from northern states. This conclusion is stated with great caution, both because the results are somewhat ambiguous and because they may be misinterpreted. While all signs of the simple correlation coefficients are as predicted (suggesting

**Table 8-9**
**Migration Elasticities of Geographic Location**

| Migration Rate | Age Categories | | |
| --- | --- | --- | --- |
| | Aged 65+ | Aged 65-69 | Aged 64- |
| Gross In-Migration | | | |
| Males | – | – | – |
| Females | – | – | – |
| Total | – | .51* | – |
| Gross Out-Migration | | | |
| Males | – | –.45* | –.43* |
| Females | – | – | –.44* |
| Total | –.37* | – | –.37* |

*Predicted sign.

that persons are attracted to southern states), only those for out-migration are significant. And only selected subgroups among the aged appear attracted to the southern states when other factors are taken into account.

An examination of "raw" migration statistics indicates that certain states classified as southern in Figure 8-1 experience among the highest in-migration rates of elderly persons in the nation; among these are Florida, New Mexico, Arizona, and California. However, extremely low in-migration rates into other southern states—Alabama, Georgia, Kentucky, Louisiana, Mississippi, South Carolina, and Texas—act to reduce the close association between southern states and in-migration.

Our reliance on a simple North-South variable probably explains the lack of a strong association between geography and in-migration. Other variables incorporating mean temperatures and rainfall should be developed, and when incorporated into a migration model probably would be significant predictors of in-migration rates.

Southern states do experience lower out-migration rates than northern states. Part of this may be attributed to a reluctance to leave pleasant climates. However, southern states which have climates pleasing enough to retard out-migration also should increase in-migration; obviously factors other than climate account for low out-migration rates in those southern states also having low in-migration rates.

## Entertainment and Recreation

The last "miscellaneous" variable included in our equations is the availability of recreation and entertainment services. Since elderly migrants can select their locations with less regard to possible sources of income than other migrants, they might be especially concerned with facilities for leisure-time activities. Their reduced attachment to the labor force and increased leisure time make this expectation reasonable.

### Definition of Variable

We measure the availability of recreation and entertainment services with the following variable:

$X_{47}$ = Proportion of the civilian labor force employed in the entertainment and recreation services industry.

This variable is used cautiously because many types of entertainment and recreation are of little interest to elderly persons while other types of activities of potentially great interest are not classified in entertainment and recreation. For example, night club entertainment and carnivals are probably of more interest to several groups of younger persons than to older persons. At the same time, public parks (city, state, and national) and home craft shops probably are of great interest to elderly persons, but neither is classified as being in the entertainment and recreation industry. We must assume that the supply of recreation services to elderly persons varies in some regular way with employment in that industry.

## Simple Correlation Coefficients

We expected that entertainment and recreation would be positively associated with in-migration rates and negatively associated with out-migration rates. The simple correlation coefficients in Table 8-10 lend scant support to this hypothesis. While the coefficients are of the expected signs for in-migration, none of those in the table is significant at even the .05 confidence level. Furthermore, the coefficients for out-migration, while not significant, are nevertheless larger than those for in-migration.

**Table 8-10**
**Simple Correlation Coefficients between Entertainment and Recreation, and Migration**

| Age Categories | In-Migration Rates | Out-Migration Rates |
|---|---|---|
| Persons Aged 65+ | .122* | .175 |
| Persons Aged 65-69 | .099* | .203 |
| Persons Aged 64- | .160* | .227 |

*Predicted sign.

## Migration Elasticities

$X_{47}$ does not appear in a single regression equation.

## Conclusions

Availability of recreation and entertainment services probably has little influence on migration rates of elderly persons. It is possible, however, that we have failed to measure adequately the relative amounts of entertainment and recreation available to the elderly in various states.

**Stability of the Migration "Mechanism"**

Implicit in our rather elaborate examination of interstate migration rates between 1955 and 1960 is the assumption that our findings would have application and relevance beyond the period covered by that data. In fact, this assumption is implicit in virtually all research which utilizes a body of data limited in time and place. We have utilized 1970 census data to study migration over the period 1965-1970 as a test of this assumption as it relates to interstate migration.

### Selection of the Variables

The first step in this testing procedure was to select a relatively small set of independent variables from the large set (63 variables) previously employed. A total of eight variables were picked—six of them because their correlation coefficients were highly significant and of the predicted signs, and because they frequently appeared in the regression equations with the same sign. Those so selected were past migration rates ($X_1$ and $X_2$), median income of the population ($X_{12}$), the proportion of elderly persons with incomes under \$3,000 ($X_{13}$), occupancy rates ($X_{53}$), and the North-South designation of a state ($X_{55}$).

But just as it is important that variables significant in the 1955-1960 period should be significant in the 1965-1970 period, those insignificant in the earlier period also should be insignificant in the latter period. If both tendencies are not verified, the implicit assumption mentioned above is invalid, and research work of this general type will have little value other than for historical perspective. Consequently, we selected two additional variables *because* they were insignificant in the 1955-1960 period and because their insignificance was unexpected. State and local per capita expenditures on welfare ($X_{63}$) was included because so many public officials act as though such expenditures are an important ingredient in the locational decision. The unemployment rate ($X_{20}$) is included because it is an important element in many migration studies of the labor force.

While the eight independent variables selected as listed above are not identical to their counterparts used in explaining migration between 1955 and 1960, if only because their observations relate to different years, they are defined in a closely parallel fashion. These variables are:

$X'_1 =$ Number of in-migrants aged five years and older

$X'_2 =$ Number of out-migrants aged five years and older, 1955-1960 divided by 1960 population aged five years and older

$X'_{12} =$ 1959-1969 average median income of all families

$X'_{13} =$ Proportion of persons aged 65 and older whose 1969 incomes were less than \$3,000

$X'_{20} =$ 1950-1960 average unemployment rate for the civilian labor force

$X'_{52} =$ Proportion of housing units occupied, 1960-1970 average

$X'_{54} =$ 1 if the majority of the land area of a state lies north of the 37th parallel; = 2 if the majority of the land area of the state lies south of the 37th parallel

$X'_{63} =$ Per capita state and local expenditures on public welfare, 1967-1971 average

Table 9-1 contains the means, standard deviations, and coefficients of variations for the eight variables defined above, and for their counterparts relating to the earlier period.

## Some Observations

The two past migration rates are higher for the later period, but this is expected, as five years, rather than one, are covered. The average of median incomes rose a little over 75 percent between the two periods of \$7,168, with a tendency toward more even distributions among the states apparent. Unemployment and occupancy rates each rose slightly. Since none of the states changed geographic location, the mean of our North-South variable is unchanged. The average of per capita state and local expenditures for welfare more than doubled, and as the coefficients of variation indicates, variation among the states was falling.

The lone surprise was an increase in the mean of the proportion of elderly persons receiving annual incomes of less than \$3,000. This result is at variance not only with our preconceived feelings as to income trends of older persons, but also with published data showing a fall in this proportion for the United States taken as a whole. The explanation for the apparent discrepancy lies in the "tricks" numbers can play on the unsuspecting. In this case, the coefficients of variation give a hint regarding how this result could be obtained. Between the two periods, this coefficient fell by more than 50 percent from 20.8 to 9.0, indicating that older persons with extremely low incomes are becoming more evenly distributed throughout the United States. This trend toward more even distribution has the tendency of raising the mean of the

**Table 9-1**
**Summary Statistics for Eight Selected Independent Variables, 1955-1960 Versus 1965-1970**

| | Mean | | Standard Deviation | | Coefficient of Variation | |
|---|---|---|---|---|---|---|
| | 1955-60 | 1965-70 | 1955-60 | 1965-70 | 1955-60 | 1965-70 |
| Past In-Migration | .033 | .046 | .020 | .048 | 61.6 | 104.3 |
| Past Out-Migration | .032 | .045 | .018 | .017 | 56.2 | 37.8 |
| Median Income | $4,069 | $7,168 | 780.736 | 1164.564 | 19.2 | 16.2 |
| Proportion of the Elderly with Incomes under $3,000 | .510 | .642 | .106 | .058 | 20.8 | 9.0 |
| Unemployment Rate | .050 | .051 | .012 | .012 | 24.0 | 23.5 |
| Occupancy Rate | .908 | .913 | .032 | .023 | 3.5 | 2.5 |
| North-South | 1.292 | 1.292 | .459 | .459 | 35.5 | 35.5 |
| Public Welfare | $24.41 | $51.09 | 10.596 | 18.722 | 43.4 | 36.7 |

proportions.[a] Evidently it has a strong enough impact to raise the calculated mean proportion of older persons with such low incomes.

### Simple Correlation Coefficients

The simple correlation coefficients relating each of the eight independent variables to each of six migration rates appear in Table 9-2.[b] Generally, we find that broad patterns observed over the 1955-1960 period persist in the 1965-1970 period. As before, the most important single determinant of migration in the current period is migration in the previous period. Elderly and non-elderly persons react very differently to income differentials in both periods. Older persons move away from high-income states, while younger persons remain in such states, and are in fact attracted to them. The attraction of the southern tier of states also persists. The influence of housing occupancy rates on both age groups appears in the 1965-1970 period as it did in the 1955-1960 period. Just as importantly, unemployment rates and per capita state and local welfare payments, which were unimportant in the earlier period, also are unimportant in the later period.

All of these observations lead us to conclude that the underlying processes of migration have remained relatively unchanged over this period.[c] The correlation coefficients are discussed in more detail in the following paragraphs.

### *Past Migration*

In general, the effects of past migration on current migration appear to have remained unchanged between the two periods. All coefficients shown in Table 9-2 are significant at the .01 level of confidence. The signs for the two periods are the same in every case. Also in every case for both periods, the coefficients

---

[a]A simple example will explain this phenomenon. Assume that there are two regions; one with a total population of 12, 4 of which are poor. The other region's population is 8, none of which is poor. The mean of the proportions of poor people is $\dfrac{4/12 + 0/8}{2}$ = .175. Now assume that 2 of the poor people from the first region move to the second. The mean of the proportions of poor people is now $\dfrac{2/10 + 2/10}{2}$ = .2 even though the total proportion of poor has not changed. Of course, movements of the rich can have the same effect.

[b]Since relatively few differences appeared when we separated migration rates by sex (none of a regular nature cutting across all independent variables) we have utilized only migration rates for "all persons" in each age group.

[c]We remind the reader that we carefully explored in earlier chapters the bases for expecting certain variables to be associated with interstate migration of the elderly, and for why the elderly might react to these variables in ways different from those of younger persons. Such discussions need not be repeated.

for past in-migration with current in-migration, and for past out-migration with current out-migration, are higher than those for past out-migration with current in-migration and for past in-migration with current out-migration. No clear pattern of increase or decrease of the coefficients over the decades can be discerned. Interpretation of these findings is not straightforward, as we discussed in Chapter 3. At the least, however, it is possible to say that the determinants of interstate migration of both elderly and non-elderly persons have continued to change only slowly, so that past observations have high predictive value.

*Public Welfare*

The public welfare variable is somewhat more powerful in explaining migration for the 1965-1970 period than it was for the 1955-1960 period. For the earlier period, none of the coefficients in Table 9-2 are significant at even the .05 confidence level. Four of the six coefficients for the later period are significant at the .05 level or higher. Unfortunately, however, the signs of these coefficients are contrary to our expectations. They indicate that high levels of public welfare expenditures discourage in-migration of elderly persons. This anomolous result probably is due to the fact that high welfare states are generally in the northeast, while low welfare states are generally in the more climatically satisfying southern regions of the country.

*Income*

The coefficients for the two selected income variables display remarkable stability between the two periods. Coefficients which are significant for the earlier time span are also significant for the later one. All of the signs remain unchanged. All of the significant coefficients for the later period are higher than the corresponding coefficients for the earlier period; these differences are not, however, statistically significant themselves.

*Unemployment Rate*

None of the coefficients for unemployment rates was significant in the earlier period, and none is significant in the current period.

*Occupancy and Geography*

The effects of housing stock occupancy and geography have, like those already discussed, remained virtually unchanged. Table 9-2 contains just a single case in

**Table 9-2**

**Simple Correlation Coefficients for Eight Selected Variables, 1955-1960 Versus 1965-1970[a]**

| Independent Variables | Gross In-Migration Aged 65+ | | Gross Out-Migration Aged 65+ | | Gross In-Migration Aged 65-69 | |
|---|---|---|---|---|---|---|
| | 1955-60 | 1965-70 | 1955-60 | 1965-70 | 1955-60 | 1965-70 |
| Past In-Migration | .783* | .972* | .518 | .500 | .759* | .972* |
| Past Out-Migration | .724 | .433 | .632* | .935* | .701 | .407 |
| Median Income | .144 | .064 | .423* | .460* | .116 | .029 |
| Proportion of the Elderly with Incomes under $3,000 | −.191 | −.292 | −.445* | −.568* | −.151 | −.264* |
| Unemployment Rate | .081 | −.051 | .114 | −.008 | .058 | −.063 |
| Occupancy Rate | −.467* | −.363* | −.268 | −.116 | −.434* | −.390* |
| North-South | .172* | .177* | −.525* | −.492* | .250* | .201* |
| Public Welfare | −.170 | −.357 | −.161* | −.117* | −.161 | −.341 |

which a significant coefficient for one period is not matched by a corresponding significant coefficient in the other period. This is the case of the coefficients for the occupancy rate and gross out-migration of non-elderly persons. The coefficient still has the "wrong" sign, however. No other notable changes for these variables appear in the table.

### Continuity of Important Factors

These findings appear to mean that the migration processes we have investigated are highly stable in two senses. First, the determinants of migration themselves have remained stable, i.e., factors which previously were important are still important; those which were not important still are not important. Second, the relationships between migration and other variables have remained stable, i.e., the relative strengths of the various associations have changed little. The somewhat subtle, but critical distinction being drawn here is that between (a) the parameters or forms of a set of structural equations, and (b) the values of the exogenous variables.

It is conceivable, for example, that the structural equations of the migration process could remain unchanged (as shown by the stability of the coefficients

| Gross Out-Migration Aged 65-69 | | Gross In-Migration Aged 64- | | Gross Out-Migration Aged 64- | |
|---|---|---|---|---|---|
| 1955-60 | 1965-70 | 1955-60 | 1965-70 | 1955-60 | 1965-70 |
| .491 | .360 | .921* | .839* | .736 | .494 |
| .619* | .878* | .877 | .474 | .838* | .670* |
| .510* | .592* | .170 | .032 | −.175 | −.221 |
| −.515* | −.614* | −.174 | −.206 | .212 | −.034 |
| .133 | −.022 | .029 | −.188* | .081 | −.129 |
| −.215 | .023 | −.342* | −.374* | −.221 | −.345 |
| −.575* | −.571* | .131* | .072* | −.100* | −.082* |
| −.096* | −.007* | −.039 | −.335 | −.015 | −.356 |

aCoefficients with expected signs are identified by an asterisk (*); those significant at the .05 level of confidence by a single underscore, and those significant at the .01 level of confidence by a double underscore.

for the income, public sector, and miscellaneous variables) and yet the patterns of migration could have changed drastically (this would be shown, if it occurred, by low coefficients linking past and current migration rates). Such a thing could happen if the state variations in income, housing occupancy and public sector variables had changed dramatically. Our results show, however, that such major shifts in the values of determinants of migration have not occurred. This means that migration of elderly persons is relatively easy to predict.

As a first approximation, it is reasonable to forecast that for any fairly long period in the future, the rates of in- and out-migration of elderly persons will be similar to such rates for a similar period in the past. Such a first approximation can be improved slightly by taking account of such minor changes in the values of factors influencing migration which are likely to occur. This can be done by use of various slope coefficients relating migration to these influencing variables. We now turn to a discussion of these coefficients.

### Migration Elasticities

Results of the regressions involving the selected independent variables and migration rates are displayed in Table 9-3. The coefficients of determination in

**Table 9-3**
**Migration Equations for the Period 1965-1970**

| Migration Rate | $R^2$ | Constant | Gross In-Mig. | Gross Out-Mig. | Median Income | % Low Income | Unemp. Rate | % Occ. Housing | North-South | Per Cap. Pub. Welfare |
|---|---|---|---|---|---|---|---|---|---|---|
| **Gross In-Migration** | | | | | | | | | | |
| Persons Aged 65+ | .95 | 1.6168 | .9202 (269.34) | -.0112 (.02) | -.1416 (.33) | -.0663 (.03) | .0888 (.88) | -.8517 (.78) | -.0358 (.01) | -.1192 (2.42) |
| Persons Aged 65-69 | .96 | 3.0629 | 1.0018 (315.08) | -.0708 (.66) | -.3385 (1.83) | -.0431 (.01) | .0272 (.08) | -1.2224 (1.58) | -.0917 (.59) | -.0505 (.43) |
| Persons Aged 64- | .76 | -.0389 | .5061 (38.75) | .1039 (27.66) | -.0810 (.05) | .5735 (.98) | -.2113 (2.36) | -1.2136 (.75) | -.1101 (.41) | -.0009 (.00) |
| **Gross Out-Migration** | | | | | | | | | | |
| Persons Aged 65+ | .93 | -3.3024 | .0321 (.62) | .8555 (182.92) | .3621 (4.00) | -.3783 (1.69) | .1561 (5.10) | .2434 (.12) | .1045 (.09) | .0018 (.00) |
| Persons Aged 65-69 | .91 | -7.5769 | -.0479 (.75) | .9639 (127.38) | .8537 (12.19) | -.2472 (.40) | .1402 (2.26) | .9760 (1.05) | .1542 (1.74) | .0383 (.26) |
| Persons Aged 64- | .72 | 9.0172 | .1338 (3.31) | .5987 (.66) | -1.0603 (10.59) | -.1657 (.10) | -.1108 (.79) | .1810 (.02) | .0519 (.11) | .0240 (.06) |

$F$-values ( ).

these equations are about as high as those obtained in the larger study of the 1960 data.[d] The particular coefficients of the equations and the migration elasticities of the individual variables are, of course, not directly comparable to those of (in) the equations discussed in Chapters 3 through 8. The reason is that many variables appear in those equations which were not considered here. Furthermore, a few minor differences in definition of the variables were inevitable. The most notable of which involves the previous migration variables $(X'_1$ and $X'_2)$. For study of the 1955-1960 period, the only available previous migration variables related to the 1949-1959 period. For 1965-1970 migration, we could obtain only migration in the 1955-1960 period for our measure of previous migration.

## Conclusions

Generally speaking, our observations relating to the migration elasticities as discussed throughout Chapters 3 through 8 are still relevant, and we will not bore the reader by repeating them here. Several overall observations, however, should be made. First, the migration elasticities accompanying past in- and past out-migration rates are higher and more significant for older persons than for younger persons. This suggests that interstate migration patterns of the elderly are substantially more stable than those of the young.

Second, the elderly react differently to median income levels than do younger persons. The out-migration elasticities for both "all persons" over age 65 and those aged 65-69 are positive; that for persons aged 64 and under is negative. In all three equations these elasticities are statistically significant.

We reach the general conclusion from our comparison of 1965-1970 and 1955-1960 statistical results that the migration mechanisms are reasonably stable. Therefore, the findings we have reported throughout the empirical portions of this book are relevant not only to the 1955-1960 period. Rather, these results have broader implications for the 1970s and beyond. Naturally, we do not rule out the possibility that important structural changes will occur. Rising costs of food and travel, changing age distribution of the population, changing government policies concerning income distribution, and other possible alterations in the environment could cause dramatic changes in migration patterns. We observe, however, that the character of migration of elderly persons during these two recent five-year periods, separated by another five-year period, was remarkably stable.

---

[d]Those relating to gross in-migration and gross out-migration rates of younger persons are lower because we selected variables of particular relevance to the elderly. We feel confident that inclusion of several additional variables more relevant to younger persons would have brought the $R^2$s up to those achieved in earlier chapters.

# 10 Summary and Conclusions

In this book we have analyzed the impact individually and jointly of a number of forces which might influence migration decisions of the elderly. While we concentrated our efforts on migration decisions of older persons, we also compared the migration decisions of this group with those of younger persons in an attempt to find if significant differences exist in the ways the two groups react to the same forces. These differences were discovered, and in our opinion are substantial enough to justify continued study of migration patterns of the elderly as a group distinct from younger persons.

Many of our a priori hypotheses concerning the relative strength and the nature of the forces influencing migration patterns and overall mobility of older persons were substantiated. We found that it is possible to build equations using economic data which explain very closely the variation in interstate migration rates of this group. Previously, much of the emphasis has been on sociological data. Other a priori hypotheses were not verified. The biggest surprise in this respect came in the apparently minor influence exerted by the public sector variables examined in Chapter 5. We found a high degree of long-term stability in what might be termed the "migration mechanism," a stability which confirms the use of current independent variables to predict future population movements.

We dealt with substantial aggregates, and studied only interstate migration (as opposed to intrastate or even intraurban movements) first for the period 1955-1960, and then briefly for that between 1965 and 1970. The nature of the data utilized and the timing of the beginning of our research prevented our selecting a more current period, but we feel that use of 1955-1960 as an initial starting point for extended studies of the ways in which the elderly make their locational decisions is reasonable. Subsequent research can build on the base laid by this work and compare migration patterns of later periods with these earlier patterns. Also, since the factors which influence migration decisions of the elderly population are unlikely to change drastically over even a period of 10 years, conclusions reached concerning the relative importance of these factors and the manner in which they influence decisions are still valid. (Of course, their objective values will have changed.)

A brief review of the major conclusions and implications from Chapters 4-9 follows.

132

### Review of Previous Chapters

*Past Migration*

We find that past migration patterns of elderly persons are a powerful determinant of current migration patterns. Whether this is the result of flows of information, "pull" of friends and relatives, or merely a continuation of past attractions (whatever they may have been) has not been determined.

If the close relationship between current and past migration results from flows of information, states could influence current and future migration rates by increasing the information flow. If, rather, the relationship stems from a mere continuation of past influences that change only slowly, states have little hope of exercising measurable short-run impact on interstate migration decisions. As Chapter 9 suggests, this latter alternative is a real possibility. Past migration rates have the highest correlation coefficients, and are by far the most powerful and consistent variables in the regression equations in both migration periods.

*Public Sector*

Few public sector variables seem related to migration patterns of the elderly. In fact, elderly persons were moving at a more rapid rate into states which maintained relatively strict OAA eligibility residency requirements (most of which have now been eliminated) and which spent relatively large amounts on education, than they were moving into other states with more favorable (for elderly persons) conditions in these respects. Also, elderly persons failed to be attracted to states with relatively generous income and property tax exemption, with high maximum OAA benefits, or with relatively low per capita property and income tax revenues.

The only public sector variable influencing the behavior of the elderly as predicted is per capita property tax revenues. While high per capita property tax collections do not inhibit in-migration of older persons, they do encourage more rapid out-migration.

Lack of information about state and local tax levels, public welfare provisions, availability of health care, etc., may explain why these variables have little or no association with in-migration rates. Since the decision to migrate *to* a state is made at a distance and with imperfect information, while the decision to migrate *from* a state is made in the proximity of the conditions being faced, it is understandable why high per capita property tax levels might fail to reduce in-migration, but act to increase out-migration. A known high tax rate is more compelling in the location decision than some unknown low tax rate.

Differences in the amount of information available as a possible explanation for the lack of in-migration response is supported by data in Table 5-10, which

133

showed that public sector variables "explain" only 17 percent of the variation in in-migration rates of elderly persons, but explain 27 percent of the variation in out-migration rates. Clearly these factors are acting more strongly on the decision to move from, than on the decision to move to a state. Differences in the amount of available information seems the most logical explanation.[a] States thus might be able to influence migration rates by broader dissemination of information concerning taxes, living expenses, public services available, etc.

*Incomes*

Migration rates of elderly persons are positively associated with income levels. Persons aged 65 and over move into and out of states at a more rapid rate when median incomes are high than when they are low. While younger persons also are attracted to states with high median incomes, unlike older persons they are less likely to leave the higher-income states. Conversely, older persons are less likely to leave low-income states.

Thus differences in migration reactions of younger and older persons to income levels act to increase the proportion of low-income elderly persons in low-income states and increase the proportion of high-income elderly persons in high-income states. States which can least afford to help support their elderly population, then, are the ones most likely to be asked to provide that support. Put another way, differences in migration patterns of young and old persons act to make the wealthy states wealthier and the poor states poorer.[b]

Increases in social security payments are not likely to remedy this general tendency of migration to widen state income differentials. As long as older persons with higher incomes retain their relatively greater mobility (and, of course, increases in social security will reduce, rather than increase mobility barriers) migration of this age group will act to increase average incomes of the elderly in the states to which they move and decrease average incomes in those states from which they move. Current interest in improving private pension plans also has long-run implications for mobility rates of older persons.[c]

[a]This possibility also is supported by our personal experiences. A local organization of older persons requested information from us concerning tax advantages different states offered the elderly. If an organized group finds it difficult to ferret out this type of information, it must be all but impossible for the individual to do so.

[b]The action of migration on interstate income differentials of the elderly is not contrary to our observation in Chapter 9 that such income differences are narrowing. Other factors, such as varying rates of income gains by low income elderly persons among the states could counteract this tendency. But even if neutralized by other changes, the impact of migration *by itself* is to widen such differentials.

[c]Of course, it also will influence the *overall* operation of labor markets as portability provisions become more common.

## Wage Incomes

Elderly persons react differently in their migration decisions to wage levels than do young persons. Specifically, younger persons are attracted to states with relatively high wages and repelled from states with relatively low wages. Elderly persons, however, discriminate between industry wage rates. They are attracted to states with high wage incomes in service industries, but repelled from those with high wages in manufacturing.

The explanation for this may lie with older persons' view (or experiences) concerning relative job opportunities. High wages in service industries could represent higher income expectations since these industries are comprised of relatively more jobs for which the elderly are likely to be employed, whereas high wages in manufacturing could represent simply higher costs of living not offset by increased wage expectations.

Our data are not well suited for testing such speculations, since we do not know the employment patterns by age and industry for each state, nor do we know actual wage rates. These data can be developed, however, and when available would throw a great deal of light not only on migration response to wage income possibilities, but also the labor-force participation response to such variations.

## Labor-Force Variables

Results from individual labor-force variables are confusing to say the least. Our hypothesis (consistent with scattered evidence from other research) for these variables is that elderly persons with a looser attachment to the labor force are more mobile than others with a tighter attachment. Thus states in which elderly persons have low participation rates, high labor-force turnover rates, and work only a small proportion of a year should be states with high in- and high out-migration rates.

Some of our evidence is consistent with these hypotheses. Multiple regression equations suggest that in-migration of elderly persons is positively related to low participation rates, to high turnover rates, and to a tendency of older persons to work less than 13 weeks a year. Out-migration is seen to be negatively related to participation rates.

It is not clear, however, whether these labor-force variables are in fact the independent variables influencing migration as the regression technique assumes, or the dependent variables influenced by migration. To determine which is the case requires that data be built from individuals rather than from aggregates.

These conclusions from discussions of income levels, wage incomes, and labor-force activity of older persons suggest that alternate solutions to the low income problem of the elderly have widely differing implications for mobility levels of this age group. It was seen earlier, for example, that increased migration rates are associated with increased incomes, so that increases in incomes achieved through transfer payments of various kinds will increase mobility. If, however, incomes are raised by improving older persons' access to the labor market through decreases in wage-income restrictions under social security or through reductions in labor-market discrimination, it is not a foregone conclusion that mobility will increase. Increased incomes will tend to reduce mobility. The relative strength of these opposing forces on mobility is, of course, unknown. This is a question only research can resolve.

## Contiguous Population

States with small populations relative to populations in contiguous states experience relatively high out-migration rates. This may partially account for the surprisingly high out-migration rates observed in Arizona and Nevada (Table 4-1); both states have relatively small populations and border on California. There is little evidence that having surrounding states with large population pools to draw from increases gross in-migration rates for the "surrounded" state.[d]

It is not known why persons migrate from states with small populations relative to their neighbors at a more rapid rate than persons in states not so situated. The "gravity" hypotheses offer inadequate explanations for this phenomenon, and as far as we know, satisfactory alternative explanations have not yet been offered.

## North-South

The geographic variable used to indicate pleasantness of climate—a simple North-South classification—really is unable to differentiate sufficiently among the states. It was powerful enough, however, to detect an attraction of the southern states for older persons, especially those aged 65 through 69, and to detect the general reluctance of all population groups to move from the South to the North in both time periods covered by our research.

Temperature, humidity, and rainfall variables developed from selected regions of each state probably would account for more of the movement into selected southern states than did the binary variable utilized here.

---

[d]Simple correlation coefficients (Table 8-2) relating migration rates between younger persons and relative populations in contiguous states indicated that such a relationship exists, but it is not significant in the multiple regression equations.

*Recreation and Entertainment*

Availability of recreation and entertainment suffered from even greater measurement and statistical problems than the North-South variable. The meager evidence coming from the migration equations, however, suggests that persons aged 65-69 are attracted to states with relatively larger entertainment and recreation sectors.

We are not sure what improvements might be made to better measure the recreation attractions of states for the elderly. Counting attendance at state and national parks is a possibility, but this measure also has serious deficiencies.

*Rental and Occupancy Rates*

Rent levels, which were used as an index of relative living costs in different states, suggest that elderly persons move away from states where costs of living are relatively high. But relatively high living costs do not seem to deter in-migration. High occupancy rates, however, do reduce in-migration rates.

Persons under age 65 behave much the same as those over age 64 with respect to these two variables. Both groups move more slowly into states where occupancy rates are high and move more rapidly from states where rental rates are high.

The difference between thse two groups lies in the strength of their reactions. Older persons seem to be affected more strongly by both factors than younger persons.

Areas experiencing rapid growth characterized by low vacancy rates and rapidly rising housing costs, then, are likely to be relatively unattractive to the elderly. Migration patterns would tend to reduce the proportion (or retard the rate of increase in the proportion) of elderly persons living in such areas.

*Education*

Simple correlation coefficients suggest that both in- and out-migration rates of the elderly are positively associated with the education level of states' populations, but that only in-migration rates of younger persons are so related. Multiple regression equations for gross migration rates do not contain the education variable in any regular pattern, but net migration equations weakly suggest that net migration is positively associated with education levels.

This variable is not well suited to the types of data utilized in this research effort first because the education levels of elderly persons are substantially different from those of younger persons, and second because the influence of education on migration is closely intertwined with that of income and occupation. The first deficiency can be remedied by using data on individuals. The second is a continuing problem with the regression technique.

## Overall Results, Conclusions

While we place only limited confidence in specific regression coefficients, we believe that several interesting comparisons of the overall regression results can be made.

### In-Migration versus Out-Migration

First, notice from Table 10-1 that the coefficients of determination ($R^2$s) of the equations for in-, out-, and net migration differ systematically for persons aged 65 and older, and for persons aged 65 through 69. The coefficients for all in-migration equations for these age groups exceed .96. The coefficients of the out-migration equations lie between .78 and .92 (inclusive). The coefficients for net migration rates range between .89 and .95. These results can be interpreted to mean that in-migration is easier to predict than is out-migration. In behavioral terms, the higher $R^2$s for in-migration equations may mean that when individuals migrate, they are drawn to states with favorable characteristics more than they are driven from states with unfavorable characteristics. The systematic differences between the $R^2$s for in- versus out-migration equations narrowed in the 1965-1970 period, but did not disappear.

### Males versus Females

Only minor differences in $R^2$s are evident between equations for males and those for females. This is true for each of the four age groups (ages 65+, 65-69, 70+, and 64-). Apparently, variables adopted in this research explain migration of males and females equally well.

While identical variables do not appear in the "paired" migration equations for males and females for each migration rate and population group, there is substantial overlap of specific variables and near duplication of the groups of variables by type (i.e., public sector variables, labor-force variables, etc.). This suggests that the influences acting on migration decisions of (elderly) males and females are similar enough so that one "model of migration" probably can be applied to both groups even though there is a relatively high proportion of one-member households among persons aged 65 and over. It was for these reasons we used age-group totals in examining migration between 1965 and 1970.

**Table 10-1**
**Overall Regression Results ($R^2$s)**

| Age Classification | Migration Rates and Groups | | | | | | | | | | |
|---|---|---|---|---|---|---|---|---|---|---|---|
| | 1955-1960 In-Migration | | | 1965-1970 | 1955-1960 Out-Migration | | | 1965-1970 | 1955-1960 Net-Migration | | |
| | Male | Female | Total | Total | Male | Female | Total | Total | Male | Female | Total |
| 65+ | .97 | .97 | .98 | .95 | .81 | .82 | .78 | .93 | .92 | .89 | .95 |
| 65-69 | .97 | .99 | .96 | .96 | .87 | .92 | .90 | .91 | .95 | .92 | .93 |
| 70+ | – | – | – | – | – | – | – | – | .94 | .89 | .90 |
| 64- | .93 | .95 | .96 | .76 | .92 | .94 | .94 | .72 | .76 | .85 | .84 |

## Old versus Young

Most of the variables have been defined to relate to older persons (and a few of these age-specific variables do enter the regression equations for younger persons).[e] Even so, the $R^2$s of the equations relating to younger persons are as high as those relating to older persons in the earlier of the two periods we studied.[f] For the most part, these high $R^2$s are achieved through three kinds of variables—past migration, wage incomes, and labor force.

While other types of variables enter migration equations of older persons with greater frequency than they do those of younger persons, wage and income, and labor-force variables are evident in these equations with surprising regularity (given our preconception that the elderly are more concerned with leisure activities). The importance of variables relating to economic activity in the equations for persons aged 65 and over suggests that older persons remain more firmly attached to the labor force than previously thought. The relatively low participation rates observed for these persons apparently is deceptive, coming largely from the discouraged-worker effect, the wage income restrictions placed by social security, and by the observed tendency for the elderly to reduce their "work year" by reducing the number of weeks they work rather than by lowering the number of hours they work each week.[g]

While wage and income, and labor-force variables apparently are important in the migration decisions of older persons as well as younger persons, it was seen in previous chapters that reactions of older persons to specific wage and income variables differ markedly from those of younger persons in many respects. Consequently, changes in wage rates, income levels, and employment opportunities are going to change the age distribution of the population in various states.

Finally, we are convinced by the evidence presented in Chapter 9 that our conclusions possess validity beyond the basic period of study. Variables which had significant relationships with migration of elderly persons for the 1955-1960 period continue to have significant relationships for the 1965-1970 period. Therefore, we believe that policymakers and planners can rely in the near future on the results we have obtained. We offer the obvious caveat that such reliance should be tempered by reasoned consideration of the recent remarkable (even incredible) shifts in the political, social, and economic climate in the United States.

---

[e] Spurious correlation with variables not in the study probably accounts for this.

[f] Wage incomes were excluded in the equation for the 1965-1970 period and may account for the low $R^2$s in the migration equations for younger persons shown in Tables 9-3 and 10-1.

[g] A simple (and unrealistic) example illustrates this last point. Assume that in one state all elderly persons work full time four months a year and that the number working at any one time is distributed evely throughout the year. Assume that in a second state all elderly persons work one-third of a week year round. The labor-force participation rate in the first state will be 33 percent; that in the second, 100 percent.

# Bibliography

# Bibliography

Bechter, Dan M. "The Retirement Decision: Social Pressures and Economic Trends." *Monthly Review*. Federal Reserve Bank of Kansas City. (November 1972), 14-23.

Becker, Gary S. *Human Capital*. New York: National Bureau of Economic Research, 1964.

Bowen, William G., and Finegan, T. Aldrich. *The Economics of Labor Force Participation*. Princeton, New Jersey: Princeton University Press, 1969.

Brennan, Michael J.; Taft, Philip; and Schupack, Mark B. *The Economics of Age*. New York: W.W. Norton & Company, Inc., 1967.

Bultena, Gordon, and Wood, Vivian. "Normative Attitudes Toward the Aged Role Among Migrant and Nonmigrant Retirees." *The Gerontologist* 9, 3 (1969): 204-08.

Bureau of Business Sources. *Study of Migration*. Tempe: Arizona State University, 1958.

Chen, Yung-Ping. "Income Tax Exemptions for the Aged as a Policy Instrument." *National Tax Journal*. National Tax Association, 16 (December 1963): 325-36.

Davis, Harry E. "Pension Provisions Affecting the Employment of Older Workers." *Monthly Labor Review* 97, 4 (April 1973): 41-45.

Dwight, Donald R. "State and Local Resources Allocation and the Aging." *The Gerontologist* 10, 3 (1970): 202-06.

Eteng, William Inya A., and Marshall, Douglas G. *Retirement and Migration in the North Central States. A Comparative Analysis: Wisconsin, Florida, Arizona*. Population Series No. 20. Department of Rural Sociology. College of Agricultural and Life Sciences. Madison: University of Wisconsin, March 1970.

Giest, Harold. *The Psychological Aspects of Retirement*. Springfield, Ill.: Charles C. Thomas, Publisher, 1968.

Goldstein, Sidney. "Socio-Economic and Migration Differentials Between the Aged in the Labor Force and in the Labor Reserve." *The Gerontologist* 7, 1 (1967): 31-40.

Greenwood, Michael. "Lagged Response in the Decision to Migrate." *Journal of Regional Science* 10, 3 (December 1970): 375-84.

Honnen, James S.; Eteng, William Inya A.; and Marshall, Douglas G. *Retirement and Migration in the North Central States. Comparative Socioeconomic Analysis: Wisconsin and Florida*. Population Series No. 19. Department of Rural Sociology. College of Agricultural and Life Sciences. Madison: University of Wisconsin, July 1969.

Jaffe, A.J. "Consumers Without Income." *The Aging Consumer. Occasional Papers in Gerontology*. No. 8, *Papers from the 22nd Annual Conference on*

*Aging.* Institute of Gerontology. Ann Arbor, Michigan: University of Michigan Press, 1969, 27-39.

Langford, Marilyn. *Community Aspects of Housing for the Aged.* Center for Housing and Environmental Studies. Ithaca, N.Y.: Cornell University, 1962.

Lansing, John B., and Mueller, Eva. *The Geographic Mobility of Labor.* Survey Research Center. Institute for Social Research. Ann Arbor: University of Michigan Press, 1967.

Manley, Charles R. "The Migration of Older People." *American Journal of Sociology* 59 (January 1954): 324-31.

Metropolitan Life Insurance Company. "Living Arrangements and Mobility of the Aged." *Statistical Bulletin* 41 (August 1960): 6-8.

Miller, Ann Ratner. *Net Intercensal Migration to Large Urban Areas of the United States.* Population Studies Center. Philadelphia: University of Pennsylvania, May 1964.

Morgan, James N. "Trends in Early Retirement." *The Aging Consumer. Occasional Papers in Gerontology.* No. 8, *Papers from the 22nd Annual Conference on Aging.* Institute of Gerontology. Ann Arbor, Michigan: University of Michigan Press, 1969, 41-45.

Nelson, Phillip. "Migration, Real Income and Information." *Journal of Regional Science* 1 (Spring 1959): 43-62.

Prasad, S. Benjamin. "The Retirement Postulate of the Disengagement Theory." *The Gerontologist* 4 (March, 1964), 20-23.

_____, and Johnson, Alton C. "Residential Mobility of the Retired Industrial Worker." *Land Economics* 40 (May 1964): 220-23.

Riley, Matilda White, and Foner, Anne. *Aging and Society.* Vol. 1: *An Inventory of Research Findings.* New York: Russell Sage Foundation, 1968.

Shatto, Gloria M., ed. *Employment of the Middle-aged: Papers from Industrial Gerontology Seminars.* Springfield, Ill.: Charles C. Thomas Publisher, 1972.

Sheldon, Henry D. "The Changing Demographic Profile." *Handbook of Social Gerontology.* Clark Tibbits, ed. Chicago: University of Chicago Press, 1960.

Shyrock, Henry S., Jr. *Population Mobility Within the United States.* Community and Family Study Center. Chicago: University of Chicago Press, 1964.

Simkins, Paul D. "Regional Differences in the Recent Migration to Arizona." (Abstract). *Association of American Geographers* 52 (Summer 1962): 360.

Sjaastad, Larry A. "The Relationship Between Migration and Income in the United States." *Papers and Proceedings of the Regional Science Association* 6 (1960): 37-64.

Thurow, Lester C., and Lucas, Robert E.G. "The American Distribution of Income: A Structural Problem." A Study prepared for the Joint Economic Committee, U.S. Congress, 92d Cong., 2d sess. Washington, D.C.: G.P.O., 1972.

Tiebout, Charles. "A Pure Theory of Local Expenditures." *Journal of Political Economy* 64 (October 1956): 416-24.

U.S. Department of Agriculture. Economic Research Service. *Net Migration of the Population. 1950-1960.* Vol. 1. Washington, D.C.: G.P.O., 1965.

U.S. Department of Commerce. Bureau of the Budget. *Compendium of State Government Finances in 1950.* Washington, D.C.: G.P.O., June 1951.

————. *Compendium of State Government Finances in 1957.* Washington, D.C.: G.P.O., May 1958.

————. *Compendium of State Government Finances in 1962.* Washington, D.C.: G.P.O., May 1963.

————. Bureau of the Census. *Current Population Reports.* Series P-20, No. 262, "Mobility of the Population of the United States: March 1970 to March 1973." Washington, D.C.: G.P.O., 1974.

————. *Current Population Reports*, Series P-23, No. 43, "Some Demographic Aspects of Aging in the United States." Washington, D.C.: G.P.O., 1973.

————. *1950 Census of Housing.* Vol. 1. Washington, D.C.: G.P.O., 1952.

————. *1950 Census of Population.* Vol. 2. *Characteristics of the Population.* Washington, D.C.: G.P.O., 1952.

————. *1950 Census of Population.* Special Reports. *Population Mobility-States and State Economic Areas.* Washington, D.C.: G.P.O., 1956.

————. *1960 Census of Population.* Vol. 1. *Characteristics of the Population.* Washington, D.C.: G.P.O., 1961.

————. *1960 Census of Population.* Vol. 2. *Characteristics of the Population.* Washington, D.C.: G.P.O., 1961.

————. *1960 Census of Population. Evaluation and Research Program of the U.S. Censuses of Population and Housing, 1960: Effects of Interviewers and Crew Leaders*, Series ER-60, No. 7. Washington, D.C.: G.P.O., 1968.

————. *1960 Census of Population.* Special Reports. *Mobility for States and State Economic Areas: Final Report.* Washington, D.C.: G.P.O., 1962.

————. *1970 Census of Population.* Vol. 1. *Characteristics of the Population.* Washington, D.C.: G.P.O., 1971.

————. *1970 Census of Population.* Subject Reports. *Employee Status and Work Experience: Final Report.* Washington, D.C.: G.P.O., 1973.

U.S. Department of Health, Education and Welfare. "Florida Tops Iowa in 65+ Ratio." *Aging* 165 (July 1968): 16-17.

U.S. Department of Labor. *Manpower Report of the President.* Washington, D.C.: G.P.O., January 1969.

U.S. Senate, Special Committee on Aging. "Housing for the Elderly: A Status Report." 93d Cong. 1st sess. Washington, D.C.: G.P.O., 1973.

White House Conference on Aging. *Aging in the States.* Washington, D.C.: G.P.O., January 1961.

White House Conference on Aging. *Protective and Social Support.* Washington, D.C.: G.P.O., 1971.

# Index

# Index

## About the Authors

**Steve L. Barsby** is a director of economic research for a national trade association in Washington, D.C. He received the Ph.D. from the University of Oregon in 1968, and taught at the University of Arizona during the period 1967-1972. His previous publications include one book, *Cost-Benefit Analysis and Manpower Programs*, and several articles in the professional literature.

**Dennis R. Cox** is an economist for the United States Department of the Treasury. He received the Ph.D. in economics from Stanford University and taught at the University of Arizona from 1967 to 1972.